Hostile

Environment

GWENDOLYN MINK

CORNELL UNIVERSITY PRESS *Ithaca & London*

Hostile

ENVIRONMENT

The Political Betrayal of Sexually Harassed Women

First published 2000 by Cornell University Press

Printed in the United States of America

Library of Congress Cataloging-in-Publication Data

Mink, Gwendolyn, 1952–
  Hostile environment : the political betrayal of sexually harassed women / Gwendolyn Mink.
      p.   cm.
    Includes bibliographical references and index.
    ISBN 0-8014-3644-3 (cloth)
    1. Sexual harassment—Law and legislation—United States.   2. Sexual harassment—Political aspects—United States.   3. Sexual harassment—Government policy—United States.   I. Title.

KF3467 .M56 1999
342.73'0878—dc21   99-046800

Cornell University Press strives to use environmentally responsible suppliers and materials to the fullest extent possible in the publishing of its books. Such materials include vegetable-based, low-VOC inks, and acid-free papers that are recycled, totally chlorine-free, or partly composed of nonwood fibers. Books that bear the logo of the FSC (Forest Stewardship Council) use paper taken from forests that have been inspected and certified as meeting the highest standards for environmental and social responsibility. For further information, visit our website at www.cornellpress.cornell.edu.

Cloth printing   10 9 8 7 6 5 4 3 2 1

contents

for THEODORE J. LOWI

preface

n January 1998, the world learned that President Bill Clinton might have had a fling with a White House intern, might have lied about it under oath, and might have encouraged the intern to lie as well. Any such lies would have subverted justice in Paula Jones's sexual harassment case against the president, as they would have been told in response to questions posed by Jones during formal legal proceedings. Jones's was the most visible sexual harassment litigation ever (Anita Hill never filed charges against Clarence Thomas), so allegations of perjury against the defendant and a witness in her case drew considerable public attention to sexual harassment law. The attention was mostly negative, with some people blaming the law for the fix in which the president found himself, and others blaming Paula Jones and a "vast right-wing conspiracy" for dogging the president with a weak legal claim.

The hostile tenor of public discussion of Paula Jones and Monica Lewinsky disturbed me from the beginning, as did the almost routine misrepresentation of sexual harassment law. The only voices raised in defense of Jones or Lewinsky, it seemed, were conservative ones; and while those voices pealed for the "rule of law," they did not bespeak comprehension of the significance of sexual harassment law to women's equality. Missing in the din of public debate about presidential sex and Paula Jones's sexual harassment case was a defense of the rights of sexually harassed women, an explanation of the obligations of a sexual harassment defendant, and an elucidation of sexual harassment law. Most distressing, many of the expected advocates of sexually harassed women and their law—leading feminists—entered the public debate on the side of the defendant where they interpreted the law to Jones's detriment and to the detriment of all sexual harassment plaintiffs as well.

I had never planned to write a book about sexual harassment, but the strange politics unleashed by *Jones v. Clinton* compelled me to do so. Partly, I thought that if I could demystify the law by telling the story of where it came from and what it aims to do, I might help dissipate public suspicion of the law and of the women who use it. But mostly I wanted to answer the insidious blows to sexual harassment law delivered by its erstwhile friends. Against leading feminists' all-too-convenient redefinition of what sexual harassment is and what the law guards against, I wrote *Hostile Environment* to defend the rights of sexual harassment plaintiffs so that sexual harassment law might one day recover its feminist moorings.

Although *Hostile Environment* emerged from a recent political moment, it draws its spirit from lifelong bonds forged in a long-ago struggle. I am especially indebted to Aline Kuntz, whose courage and resilience twenty years ago continue to inspire me. I am also grateful to Mark Silverstein, William Tetreault, and Jeremiah Riemer, who were irreplaceable comrades and advisers back then, as they continue to be today. I hope Isaac Kramnick knows how much I appreciate his generosity and wisdom. A great teacher, he helped me to survive turbulent times and to do so with the skills to reflect on them. He also lent me indispensable support as I wrote this book.

Another great teacher, Theodore J. Lowi, has been an indefatigable mentor and friend. My debts to him are massive. He has given me precious time, enthusiastic support, and firm but kind counsel over the years. I try to reciprocate these gifts, although I know I never will be able to do so fully. But one debt I cannot even try to repay: the measure of vindication he helped Aline and me win in the struggle that bound us all together twenty years ago. The best I can do is to gesture my gratitude by dedicating *Hostile Environment* to him.

Ted not only was a guiding spirit behind *Hostile Environment*, he also participated concretely in the book's development. The ideas that became the book emerged from our conversations and fax arguments about the Jones case and Lewinsky scandal. Once I began writing, he reviewed each chapter as I completed it—offering me, as usual, a productive mix of bountiful criticism and sparing praise. He of course bears no blame for *Hostile Environment*, but the book does bear his imprint.

Rita E. Walker, with whom I have worked on sexual harassment policy issues at the University of California at Santa Cruz, surrendered what little time she has for fun reading to pore over my somber prose. The book has benefited in innumerable ways from her policy expertise and street-level experience, just as I have benefited from her encouragement. Likewise, the book has been improved by criticism from Eileen Boris, Jessica Delgado, and Linda Thome, who each read chapters in progress. Eileen provided predictably astute and challenging comments based on her own extensive grasp of feminist legal scholarship and U.S. women's history. Jessica offered the insights of fresh legal training, while Linda generously shared her vast legal knowledge. While Rita, Eileen, Jessica, and Linda supplied me with crucial substantive guidance, they are not responsible for any errors that linger in the book, and they should not be blamed for its argument.

Sonia Alvarez and Dana Frank shored me up with their intellectual energy and moral support. As ever, I learned from our conversations about feminism and gained confidence from their interest in my work.

I've always assumed that it is the writing of manuscripts, not the publication of books, that is the real test of an author's mettle. *Hostile Environment* shattered that illusion. During the high drama of book production, Paul Kleven kept me on an even keel with his sage and sensitive counsel. Philip Mattera of the National Writers' Union answered every question I sent his way with thorough and helpful information.

As always, my parents, John and Patsy Mink, dutifully read every word I wrote, often correcting my grammar but never my point of view. I am nourished by their support for my work, especially when they do not agree with me.

I might not have dared to write *Hostile Environment* were it not for two editors and a research assistant. Cecelia Cancellaro's early support excited my interest in doing a book on sexually harassed women and the law. Peter Agree's editorial vision spurred me to make the commitment to writing the book now. Knowing that I can count on Peter for superb guidance, unstinting support, and excellent steak made the challenge of fast writing about intricate laws and breaking political events seem if not less daunting, at least worthwhile. The person who helped me forget that writing *Hostile Environment* would require staggering amounts of research in a short period of time was my assistant, Sarah Carey. She gathered all that I asked her to with impressive efficiency and accuracy. The Academic Senate's Committee on Research at the University of California at Santa Cruz made Sarah's work possible.

GWENDOLYN MINK

Santa Cruz, California

o n e Hostile Environment

When Anita Hill recounted how then-Judge Clarence Thomas had sexually harassed her, the *Wall Street Journal* speculated that she was motivated to make such a claim by her ideological opposition to the judge's conservative views.[1] On Capitol Hill, key Republican strategists questioned not only her motives but also her sanity.[2] At the Judiciary Committee hearings, one senator accused her of "flat-out

---

1. Lally Weymouth, "Some Clues to Anita Hill's Motive," *Wall Street Journal*, November 20, 1991.
2. Maureen Dowd, "Getting Nasty Early Helps GOP Gain Edge on Thomas," *New York Times*, October 15, 1991; Andrew Rosenthal, "Use of Psychiatry in the Battle Raises Ethics Issue," *New York Times*, October 20, 1991.

perjury," while another suggested she had concocted her testimony with the help of case law and excerpts from the novel *The Exorcist*.[3]

When Paula Jones told the nation that she had been sexually harassed in a Little Rock hotel room by then-Governor Bill Clinton, Michael Isikoff (who later became famous for his access to Linda Tripp and her audiotapes) reasoned in the *Washington Post* that Jones had "smelled money" in leveling charges against the President of the United States.[4] At the White House, presidential strategists portrayed Jones as a gold-digging "trailer-park floozy" who was the pawn of the Republican right wing.[5] Many of the president's friends insisted that Jones and her supporters were the *real* harassers: Jesse Jackson, for example, suspected that conservatives "want him to drop his pants in public. Paula Jones's lawyers are hardly masking their gratification at the demand for him to expose his body parts in a deposition."[6] Fighting fire with fire, meanwhile, the president's lawyer, Robert Bennett, threatened to excavate and expose Jones's sexual history, presumably to diminish her credibility and to show that even if the president did expose himself and tell her to "kiss it," she couldn't possibly have been offended.

The vicious personal attacks weathered by Anita Hill and Paula Jones are no different from those endured by many women who bring sexual harassment claims, although the attacks against Hill and Jones were far louder and more visible than most. It is disappointing but not surprising that alleged harassers try to defend themselves by discrediting the women who bring charges against them. More surprising is how ecumenical this strategy can be. On the left as well as the

3. Hendrik Hertzberg, "Leaks, Lies and the Law: What Became of the GOP's Anita Hill Conspiracy Theory?" *Washington Post*, December 1, 1991.

4. Michael Isikoff, "Clinton's Accuser 'Smelled Money' in Charges," *Washington Post*, May 6, 1994.

5. Kevin Merida, "Paula Jones's Attorney Sees Public Opinion, Coverage Shifting," *Washington Post*, January 12, 1997, quoting James Carville: "Drag a hundred dollars through a trailer park and there's no telling what you'll find"; Sidney Blumenthal, "The Friends of Paula Jones," *New Yorker* (June 20, 1994): 38ff; Bob Bennett interview, "Sexual Harassment Lawsuit Brought Against President Clinton," *All Things Considered*, NPR, May 6, 1994.

6. Henry Louis Gates, Jr., "The Naked Republic," *New Yorker* (August 25, 1997): 116.

right, friends of alleged harassers have propagated ugly speculations about women who have been brave enough to vindicate their injuries. Speculations about the motives and character of the women who use sexual harassment law, in turn, have fueled attacks on the law itself — most often by right-wingers who think the law is a boondoggle for disreputable women, but more recently also by liberals who chafe when the law is deployed against their own men. Solidarity with alleged harassers against women and against the law may be par for the course among conservatives. Among liberals — and feminists — however, it is a disturbing new development. When the law's putative champions deprive even one sexually harassed woman of its protections, they betray all sexually harassed women. When they redefine the law to exclude even one woman's injury, they betray feminism's signal legal accomplishment and compromise its future.

Sexual harassment targets first began to seek legal redress in the mid-1970s. By the mid-1980s, their right to legal redress was firmly established. The law now recognizes that unwanted, demeaning, or threatening sexual conduct can limit women's opportunities, ambitions, and rewards in workplaces and in schools — that such conduct at work or in school substitutes a woman's sex for her personhood, interposing sex between a woman and her job or education. Following this, courts consider employers vicariously liable when a supervisor (or higher authority) harasses a subordinate;[7] large groups of women have won significant settlements against pervasively hostile work environments;[8] and a sexually harassed worker whose only vi-

7. *Burlington Industries, Inc. v. Ellerth*, 524 U.S. 742 *(1998); Faragher v. City of Boca Raton*, 524 U.S. 775 (1998).

8. In the largest sexual harassment case to date, the Equal Employment Opportunity Commission sued Mitsubishi Motor Manufacturing of America on behalf of three hundred women workers who had been subjected to insulting sexual innuendo and "unwanted grabbing, groping and touching." In June 1998 Mitsubishi agreed to pay $34 million to settle the case. *Equal Employment Opportunity Commission v. Mitsubishi Motor Manufacturing of America*, Joint Motion for Entry of Consent Decree, Case No. 96–1192 (C.D., Illinois, 1998). James Miller, "Mitsubishi Will Pay $34 Million in Sexual-Harassment Settlement," *Wall Street Journal*, June 12, 1998, B4; Barnaby J. Feder, "$34 Million Settles Suit for Women at Auto Plant," *New York Times*, June 12, 1998; A12.

able alternative is to give up her job can claim that she was "constructively discharged" by her employer.[9]

The law not only recognizes the objective wrongs of sexual harassment but also proceeds from the assumption that a woman's subjective experience of sexual harassment may impair her civil rights. It permits women to tell what happened and how they were affected. A woman's account of her harassment is not proof that harassment occurred, of course: her account must be weighed against her alleged harasser's claim that he didn't do it or that she was not harmed. Yet importantly, the law begins with a woman's word.

The Paula Jones case made clear, however, that while the law of sexual harassment may begin by taking at face value a woman's description of her own harassment, the politics of sexual harassment begins by questioning whether a particular woman is to be believed. Conservatives' support for Paula Jones created the possibility that for once an alleged harassment target might enjoy the presumption of credibility among a wide public. But almost from the moment Paula Jones filed her lawsuit against Bill Clinton in May 1994, many of the feminists and liberals who had championed the development of sexual harassment law joined the chorus against her.

Comparing Paula Jones to Anita Hill, feminist columnist Anna Quindlen determined that Hill was more credible than Jones, in part because Hill had been "forced" to come forward while Jones did so voluntarily.[10] Ellen Goodman, another feminist columnist, cautioned

---

9. *Young v. Southwestern Savings and Loan Association*, 509 F. 2d. 140, 144 (5th Cir., 1975), determined that when "an employee involuntarily resigns in order to escape intolerable and illegal employment requirements" to which he or she is subjected because of race, color, religion, sex, or national origin, the employer has committed a constructive discharge in violation of Title VII. *Caldwell v. Hodgeman*, 25 Fair Empl. Prac. Cas. (BNA) 1647, 1649–50 (D. Mass., 1981), held that an offensive environment caused by sexual harassment resulted in constructive discharge entitling employee to unemployment benefits. *Weihaupt v. American Medical Association*, 874 F. 2d. 419, 426 (7th Cir., 1989) found that "an employer constructively discharges an employee . . . if it makes an employee's working conditions so intolerable that the employee is forced into an involuntary resignation."

10. Anna Quindlen, "A Tale of Two Women," *New York Times*, May 11, 1994.

that "you don't have to check your skepticism at the door of feminism . . . [Paula Jones's] original coming out party at a conservative press conference, her earlier attempt to trade money for silence . . . don't make for a perfect profile."[11] Attorney Deborah Katz, who represents plaintiffs in sexual harassment cases, warned that "whenever you look at someone bringing a case you have to look at the motives that the person may have."[12] In a similar vein, National Organization for Women President Patricia Ireland told *Time* that feminists would not "rise to the right wing's bait" and must "assess the credibility of the witness."[13] Feminists thus sent a strong signal to Paula Jones that unless she proved herself credible politically they would doubt the legal credibility of her claim. Feminist groups such as NOW did aver that Paula Jones had a right to her day in court, and NOW loudly rebuked the president's lawyer when he threatened to scour Jones's sex life for discrediting information.[14] Feminist groups and leaders, however, also stoked public speculation about Jones's motivations, truthfulness, and political associations, sending a discouraging message to women who need to use sexual harassment law.[15]

If the law now will listen to a woman's experience, it does not shield her from promiscuous public scrutiny that distorts the experience she describes. It does not defend her from suspicion that her character flaws might have led to the harassment ("Just because we're making men accountable for what goes on in hotel rooms or offices

11. Ellen Goodman, "Honk If You Believe Paula Jones?" *Washington Post*, May 14, 1994; Howard Kurtz, "The Plunge into Paulagate," *Washington Post*, May 14, 1994.

12. Deborah Katz interview, "Paula Jones Lawsuit Making for Strange Bedfellows," *Morning Edition*, NPR, May 20, 1994.

13. Richard Lacayo, "Jones v. the President," *Time* (May 16, 1994): 44ff.

14. "Statement of NOW President Patricia Ireland Calling for Fair Treatment of Jones's Suit, Questioning Right Wing Disingenuous Fervor," press release, May 6, 1994; "NOW President Patricia Ireland's Statement on *Clinton v. Jones* Supreme Court Decision," press release, May 27, 1997.

15. Many women were demoralized in the wake of the Hill-Thomas hearings, for example. See Martin Tochin, "Citing Thomas Hearings, Women Refuse to Testify," *New York Times*, October 24, 1991; Milo Geyelin, "In Anita Hill Aftermath, Some Women Now Rush to Settle Claims," *Wall Street Journal*, October 18, 1991; Susan Moffat, "Hill Case Seen as Deterring Other Women," *Los Angeles Times*, October 16, 1991.

doesn't mean that women should be absolved of all responsibility," wrote Susan Estrich in *USA Today*).[16] It doesn't protect her from the charge that her harassment must be invented because her friends aren't very nice ("It's a right-wing plot," Eleanor Smeal told Larry King).[17] And it doesn't prevent allegations that her motives are entirely mercenary ("This is about money and book contracts," Robert Bennett told *Time*).[18]

Notwithstanding advances in the law, casuistry controls how we talk about sexual harassment when it involves real people. Our casuistry works against women who complain of harassment, dampening the effects of improved legal rules and remedies on women's lives. We spend more time wondering why a woman complains of harassment than why the harasser felt entitled to harass her. We second-guess her choices — why did she agree to meet her boss for a drink? why was she alone in his office? — rather than examining how he used his power. We measure her actions and reactions against what we imagine we would have done, rather than against what she tells us her situation permitted her to do.

Sexual harassment law has brought predatory, intimidating, and humiliating sexual conduct under the scrutiny of laws that are supposed to promote equality. Rescuing such conduct from the cover of private behavior, women plaintiffs, feminist lawyers, and courts have demonstrated how certain sexual conduct enforces women's (and sometimes men's) inequality. Expanding the concept of discrimination to encompass sexual dimensions of inequality, they have forged legal weapons for fighting sexual imposition and shame. But these weapons are costly, often requiring women to pay for redress with their reputations.

Although feminists and women have won important battles in law, we have not won them where reputations are won and lost: in politics. The political premise of feminism is that we should each take seriously what women say about their lives. We may come to disbelieve a particular woman or to consider her feelings to be misdi-

16. Quoted in Katha Pollitt, "Subject to Debate (Paula Corbin Jones)," *Nation* (June 13, 1994): 824.

17. ibid.

18. Lacayo, "Jones v. the President."

rected, but we should start by listening to her story and we should fight for a legal process that permits her to tell it fully. Following this premise, feminists distinguished themselves in 1991 by "believing Anita Hill" and by demanding that the United States Senate hear her out.[19] The Hill-Thomas hearings increased public attention to sexual harassment but did not increase public support for the feminist premise. Indeed, feminists' hostility toward Paula Jones suggests that not even feminists are willing to take seriously what *all* women say about their lives or to fight for all women to receive a fair hearing.

Sexual harassment law promises remedies to complainants who can convince juries that they have been harmed. It provides assistance from the Office for Civil Rights or from the Equal Employment Opportunity Commission to complainants whose schools or employers will not help. It also rewards preventive measures by schools and employers so that girls and women will not be exposed to harm. But sexual harassment law is not self-enforcing and will not by itself end sexualized inequality in workplaces and schools. Its remedies are available only to women who successfully state a legal claim. It inspires preventive action only because employers or schools fear exposure to the law's remedies. In other words, the law gains strength from the women who use it.

If we now have laws to help us fight back against our harassers, we have to dare to use them. Few women do.[20] Who would want to endure what Anita Hill had to, even on a microcosmic scale? Who would want to be Paula Jones? Who would want to be me? Twenty-five years ago, I began a struggle against a harasser in graduate school. Sadly, the chilling political climate in which I both won and lost that struggle has not changed much.

19. Maureen Dowd, "7 Congresswomen March to Senate to Demand Delay in Thomas Vote," *New York Times*, October 9, 1991.

20. According to a 1994 study, only one in four harassed women workers (24 percent of harassed African American workers and 28 percent of harassed white workers) responded to their harassment *in any way*, whether by saying something to the harasser, talking to others about the situation, or reporting it. Gail E. Wyatt and Monika Riederle, "The Prevalence and Context of Sexual Harassment Among African American and White American Women," *Journal of Interpersonal Violence*, vol. 10 (September 1994): 314.

In the fall of 1974, I entered a doctoral program in political science at Cornell University. In some ways, my first year of graduate school was quite ordinary: the workload, competitive jealousies, and uncertainty about the future made me miserable — as they did everyone else. At twenty-two, I was groping toward my vocation but unsure of its specific contours; I knew only that I wanted eventually to write about politics. The politics I wanted to write about had been defined mainly by the politics I had lived: the antiwar movement, the civil rights movement, the labor movement, and feminism.

Entering graduate school, I thought I might want to develop expertise on East Asia, since East Asian Studies had been my major in college. I also wanted to read and think about equality, imagining that at some point I would write about struggles for social justice in the United States. These interests initially drew me to the political science fields of comparative politics, political philosophy, and American politics. Although I was more political — and so, to some minds, less scholarly — than most of my peers, my course of studies was fairly typical.

Being political got me into a bit of trouble, pretty much from the beginning. I had strong views and often acted on them, usually to protest policies of one sort or another that I considered unjust. Once, I and a small group of students pressed the government department to require faculty who had ties to the Central Intelligence Agency to disclose the nature of their activities so that students could make more informed decisions about entering into mentoring relationships with them. One of my future mentors, Theodore Lowi, denounced our demand and me with it, calling me a "McCarthyite of the Left." The faculty member most directly implicated by our demand suggested that I should be expelled from the program (I was saved by my other future mentor, political philosophy professor Isaac Kramnick, who was director of graduate studies at the time).[21]

My politics were not the only thing that was out of step with my graduate program. So was my sex. There were three or four women

21. Isaac Kramnick to author.

in each of the classes immediately ahead of mine, but in my class of twenty, only two of us were women, and by the end of my first year I was the only one left. I was quite conscious of being alone and different, isolated and on display, because many of my peers treated me or talked about me as a sexual resource, predator, or curiosity rather than as an academic colleague. According to some, I was promiscuous; to others, I was a potential lay; to still others I was sexually manipulative. One colleague, a neighbor, kept a count of the men who entered my apartment, which he claimed proved I was a slut. When I didn't reciprocate his sexual interest, another colleague speculated that someone else in my cohort must have "put the clamps on me." Once, after I had begun a relationship, still another colleague propositioned me with the taunt, "Are you monogamous?" When I appeared to be at the top of my class after a seminar that served as a hazing, some students (including the other woman in my class) claimed that I had earned my A by sleeping with each of the three professors who had team-taught the seminar.

If my sex brought me some grief, so did my race. There were even fewer people of color in the program than there were women — one African American man in my class, three in classes above, and me. I have my mother's Japanese features, although they are muted by my father's Slovakian-Lithuanian ones. Whether because my specific cultural background is visually indeterminate, or because Asians are presumed to be foreigners, my peers were curious about where I "was from." Before my politics became obvious, a couple of people interpreted my shyness as passivity and guessed that I was the daughter of a South Vietnamese general or a Taiwanese lobbyist and "probably a Republican." Sometimes my race modulated my sex, such as when one guy fancied me to be his Suzie Wong. I also withstood occasional slurs, as when one colleague called me a "dragon lady," when others complained that I was "inscrutable," and when a professor told me that there were no lessons to be drawn about U.S. politics from the anti-Chinese movement in nineteenth-century California because the Chinese are "so different."

I knew I didn't fit in, but I didn't particularly want to if that meant having to become like the people who offended me. I did, however, want to be taken seriously and to enjoy the same opportunities for professional development that everyone else had. I didn't want my sex or my race to be educational liabilities. I wanted equal opportunity in spite of who I was. I lost it within months of beginning my graduate studies.

During the winter of my first year, I attended a party for faculty and graduate students at a professor's home. There, John Untel,* a senior faculty member in one of my fields of study, made sex a condition of my education and race the obstacle to my success. Without invitation or permission, he nestled himself next to me on a sofa, moved his leg against mine, and touched my thigh. His physical proximity and gestures intimidated me — scared me, in fact — as did his institutional power over me. So I just sat there as he breathed on me, cooing that I was "exotic" and "so intelligent." After a while he said he'd like to spend time alone with me and asked me to join him for a "private dinner"—just him and me. Given his physical advances, I was pretty sure that his request to see me alone was a request for sex. At its most benign, it was a prologue to such a request.

I said no and tried to move away. He became angry, saying accusingly and repeatedly, "You don't like me." I was beside myself. I didn't want to say that I did like him, after all; yet I worried what a professor could do to a student who had offended him as personally as I had. When I told him that his talk about my not liking him was making me very uncomfortable, he began to abuse me verbally. What I remember most vividly is the spate of racial slurs he directed at me. Minutes before, I had been "exotic" and "intelligent." Now I was a pitiable and inferior "Oriental," someone who could never aspire to great heights as a thinker because my race is backward and "lacks faith" in a Judeo-Christian god. When he used my race to damn my sexual rebuff, all my doubts about my abilities and all my fears that I wasn't taken seriously seemed to be confirmed.

I didn't run screaming from the room, and although I may have shed some tears, I bore no visible scars from the encounter. But the experience gnawed at me, feeding anxieties about what it portended for my education. Given Untel's brutal reaction to my rebuff, I was

*Although the identity of the professor is a matter of public record, all references to him in this book bear this alias.

pretty sure he took my "no" for an answer; I didn't think he would hit on me again. But I was desperately troubled that he had propositioned me at all. I fretted over his reaction as well, fearing that I would never be able to overcome his condemnation of my intellect. And, frankly, I was worried that I would be punished for having offended him.

I felt that Untel's conduct meant that my relationship to those parts of the graduate program over which he had influence — and perhaps even to the program as a whole — would thenceforth pivot on how I had responded to his sexual advance, not on how I would respond to my education. I was quite prepared to pay for problems of my own making — my political stand against secret faculty associations with the CIA, for example — even if that meant I would lose a plum teaching assistantship or the favor of an esteemed professor. But I was not willing to pay for a professor's decision to violate me as a student by sexualizing the educational relationship.

I turned to two professors for help. One, a man, was my first-year adviser (and also one of the professors I allegedly had bedded to get an A). The other, a woman, had invited me once or twice to participate in a feminist reading group that met at her home. Both were approachable and seemed interested in helping students.

I didn't have a plan of action, or even a goal, really. Sexual harassment had not yet received wide public attention; it did not yet even have a name. I knew that when Untel hit on me he intruded on my rights and that when I rejected him I foreclosed some of my opportunities, but I did not have the vocabulary to describe what had happened to me as sexual harassment or to persuade anyone that it constituted discrimination based on sex.

I did have a vocabulary to express anger and fear, however. I had been reduced to my sex by someone who, directly or indirectly, was responsible for my education. I agonized about the consequences of rebuffing him. I wanted both to protect myself and to somehow prevent Untel from compromising another woman student in the future.

I tried to explain this to the two professors. Especially troubling to me were the obstacles to a full course of study in Untel's field that were now in my way. I could have dropped the field, I suppose, as it was not my major emphasis. But that seemed like an awfully big price for me to pay for someone else's bad behavior. Yet if I now was afraid to take courses from Untel, what would happen when it came time to take the written comprehensive exam in that field? There would be brackets in my knowledge. Worse, Untel would almost certainly be one of the faculty evaluating the exam. What would this do to my academic standing? How would it affect letters of recommendation I would need to get a job?

The two professors listened to what I had to say, but seemed to look at my experience from Untel's point of view. The male professor laughed off my account, saying that I was too sensitive, that these things happen, and that Untel "probably just was looking for a girlfriend." The woman professor told me that Untel probably was lonely and speculated that he had propositioned me because he had been drinking. Had Untel's behavior been more extreme — had he raped rather than touched me; had he forced rather than pressured me; or had he threatened to retaliate rather than pronounced me incapable of superior work — perhaps then one or both of the professors would have understood why the incident so distressed me.

Because neither professor understood my anxiety and anger and because their most sympathetic responses were on their colleague's behalf rather than mine, I dropped the matter. Untel's vulgar sexual advance and savage rebuke of my rejection had put me in an impossible situation; I concluded that I would only make things worse for myself by complaining about it further.

And so I chose silence. The only real action I took was to avoid Untel and his courses. This was possible because the department's curricular requirements were fairly flexible at the time. We had to demonstrate competence in whole fields of study when it came to comprehensive examinations, however, so although avoiding a senior faculty member and his courses was possible, it was not advisable.

I put off taking my comprehensive exam in Untel's field as long as I could, but eventually time ran out. As I had feared, Untel was a member of my examining committee. That meant that he would participate in drafting the exam questions and in evaluating my essays. A few days before the exam, he invited the five students scheduled to take the exam to his home to discuss Hegel. I didn't want to go. I hadn't exchanged words with him for three and a half years, and I didn't want to have to interact personally with him now. I didn't want to be around him in an informal, evening session that could easily turn social. At the same time, I knew that there were risks to not going: he might be insulted; he might take my absence as arrogance or defiance; he might hold it against me if I wrote about Hegel on the exam — or if I didn't. What had happened between us the evening he harassed me exposed me to these risks. But I also knew that by now other chickens were coming home to roost: I was perceived, probably deservedly, as one of the least deferential students in the graduate program; and my politics irritated some faculty, especially conservatives like Untel who believed that scholars should aim to understand the world, not to change it. My dearest friends convinced me that, under the circumstances, I had no choice but to attend the Hegel session.

At the end of the evening, when I was about to leave with everyone else, Untel suddenly grabbed my arm, yanked me into his bedroom, and slammed the door. We were utterly alone. As he glared at me, I wondered whether he was going rape me or beat me up. He didn't harm me physically. But backing me toward a wall, he berated me for having told two professors about his sexual advance. Although these professors had discounted my experience and my feelings when I had spoken with them several years before, at least one of them apparently had decided that my story warranted discussion with Untel. The result was that Untel now had two reasons to be angry with me.

Trapped in his bedroom and terrified, I listened to him accuse me of maligning him. Whatever I said in response led him to assail my character. He then went on to say that although he had been interested in me sexually in the past he wasn't any more because he now had a girlfriend to whom he had "pledged monogamy." Closing his tirade, he brought up the exam I was about to take. Claiming impeccable objectivity, he ordered me not to think that he would evaluate me negatively just because I had once rejected him.

As soon as I got home, I called Isaac Kramnick, whom I had trusted ever since the CIA ruckus. By now, I was prepared to abandon Untel's field even though doing so would delay my progress toward writing a dissertation. Kramnick advised me to go ahead with the exam and not to worry about anything until the results were in. I accepted the advice — reluctantly — and although distraught and distracted, I completed the day-long exam on schedule. Afterward, I was pretty sure that the exam was the worst thing I had ever written and that I might well have deserved to fail. Given my distress, though, I was not my own best judge, so my performance might have been better than I feared and I might have deserved strong praise. Instead, I received a poor but passing evaluation. I'll never know whether I was graded down by a vindictive professor, or was given the evaluation I truly had earned, or was passed to preempt a sexual harassment complaint.

I didn't contest my poor evaluation, but once again chose silence. If I hadn't, perhaps Untel wouldn't have harassed a friend of mine.

A couple of years after my second incident with Untel, he accosted my friend and fellow graduate student Aline Kuntz at a party at his home. In two or three weeks' time, she was to take her comprehensive exam in Untel's field; Untel was, again, on the examining committee. After expressing unsolicited judgment about very private details of her life, he said to her, "I want to fuck you." Brooking no rejection, he insisted that "women like her" always are sexually available. She left the party, hysterical.[22]

It was now the winter of 1980. The Equal Employment Opportunity Commission would soon issue sexual harassment guidelines, and appeals courts were beginning to treat sexual harassment as a serious violation of women's civil rights. Meanwhile, a case against Yale University had brought judicial attention to the problem of sexual harassment in education.[23] Neither Aline nor I was initially aware of these developments, but we did know that Untel was wrong to sexualize the education of women.

Aline took her comprehensive exam and did well despite everything. Once out of immediate reach of Untel's evaluative authority, she could have let things lie. But she didn't feel right doing nothing. Had Untel shown some remorse for his actions, she might have been

22. Aline Kuntz to author and various government department faculty.
23. *Alexander v. Yale*, 459 F. Supp. 1 (D. Conn., 1977); *Alexander v. Yale*, 631 F. 2d. 178 (2nd Cir., 1980).

satisfied that he would not repeat his behavior toward her or any-one else. By now, however, he had rewritten her experience, implic-itly questioning either her sanity or her veracity. Within a week of his abusive proposition, Untel had called aside her partner (a fellow graduate student) to explain that Aline had misunderstood him: Untel claimed that what he really had said was, "I bet you think I want to make it with you." He further protested that he was faithful to his girlfriend — although even so, he "wouldn't throw Aline out of bed."[24]

We were convinced that Untel would continue to harass women students as long as he could get away with it and that he would con-tinue to get away with it until he was exposed to someone with insti-tutional responsibility. We decided to bring our complaints forward jointly, so that the Cornell government department, through its chair, would have no choice but to notice Untel's pattern of sexual harassment. We thought that each of our complaints would together be more credible, since mine alone clearly had not been.

On March 7, 1980, we approached one of the department's four women faculty members for advice and support. This was the same professor who had disappointed me when I had turned to her five years earlier. We sought her assistance now, not only because as a woman — and as a feminist — she seemed more likely than most to hear us out but also because she had indicated informally that she "could believe" that Untel had hit on Aline. After lengthy discus-sions about what to do, she agreed to accompany us to a meeting with the department chair, to whom Aline and I recounted our expe-riences with Untel. Our purpose in coming forward, we said, was to inform the department of Untel's past behavior so that women grad-uate students might be spared it in the future. Our only request was for a meeting with Untel, to whom we intended to explain how dam-aging his behavior had been and from whom we wanted an apology. After wondering out loud whether we weren't overreacting ("Men make passes at my wife," he said. "She handles it.") the chair agreed to request Untel's presence at a meeting the following Monday.

Untel refused to attend that meeting. Demanding formal charges

24. Mark Silverstein, memo chronicling events, Spring 1980.

and accusing us of slander, he challenged us to take lie detector tests and threatened first to expose us in the campus newspaper and then to take us to court. We declined to file formal charges because there were no procedures for hearing them. We persisted with our grievance, however, hoping that if Untel would not take responsibility and change his behavior, then perhaps the government department faculty as a whole might take responsibility and apologize on his behalf. A firestorm ensued. For two months, it was all-consuming for faculty in the department, as well as for us.

Faculty were slow to believe us; I'm not sure the majority ever did. Some doubters changed their minds after a third woman — a respected and politically untarnished student — reported having been harassed by Untel several years earlier. Of those who believed us, few were easily persuaded that Untel's actions warranted censure or punishment. The feminist faculty member who had initially befriended us soon distanced herself, focusing her concerns on the effects of the controversy on Untel's health and family rather than the effects of his conduct on us. The other women professors stayed on the sidelines. Some male faculty members denounced us as "left-wing ideologues"; some discounted our grievance as a politically suspicious attack on a conservative professor. Others tried to scare us off, admonishing that we would be professionally blacklisted and forever branded as troublemakers if we persisted with our complaints. Although he eventually became our advocate, the new director of graduate studies initially told me that my track record as a politial agitator cast doubt on my motives and my truthfulness. He warned that I would be haunted by suspicion when I tried to get a job.

Only three faculty believed us outright and grasped the harm of Untel's behavior. With Isaac Kramnick away in California that year, only one faculty member supported us sufficiently to take risks on our behalf. Theodore Lowi was now chair of my dissertation committee. I have never forgotten how my insides quaked when Aline and I met with him to explain what had happened to us and why we had complained officially about it. Although Lowi and I had a strong — if sometimes combative — working relationship, I had never told him about Untel. I had feared that he wouldn't believe me and that our relationship would collapse from the weight of his disbelief. Such fears turned out to be misplaced. He listened to us and believed, listened to Untel and still believed. And once he fully comprehended what had happened to us, he exploded in wave after wave of rage. His rage forced the department to confront Untel's conduct, which he considered an abuse of power "tantamount to rape." His role was decisive: as a distinguished senior faculty member, he could command departmental attention as we could not. Without his interventions, our complaints would have been dismissed as fabricated or imagined; and without his fierce support, my future as a political science scholar would have disappeared.

Lowi's involvement shaped the resolution of our grievance, but it did not exactly speed that resolution. Even after he made plain his support for us, the department resisted providing us the apology we sought. The department chair's priority was to preserve peace among faculty; he wanted to resolve matters quietly by faculty consensus. Untel blocked any possibility of consensus, however, as he denied that there was anything to resolve. The result was prolonged dissension, leading to a complete and irremediable rupture in relations among some faculty. Strife inside the department affected collegial relations far beyond Cornell: at other institutions, Untel's friends rallied to his support. Some impugned our credibility. One, prominent conservative thinker Allan Bloom of the University of Chicago, went so far as to shun Lowi — a friend and former colleague — because he did not take Untel's side.[25]

A full month into the controversy, the only official action proposed in response to our complaints was a code of conduct that "disapprove[d] unsolicited propositions from faculty to students" and spelled out ethical standards for faculty-student romances. We thought departmental legislation to curb faculty abuses of power was a good idea, yet its focus on romance, rather than on harassment, limited its relevance to our grievance. Frustrated, we sought assistance from the university's ombudsperson. When she demurred because we had no tangible proof that we had been harassed, we redoubled our efforts to secure some measure of justice at the department level. By now justice required not only a formal apology

25. Theodore Lowi to author.

for Untel's sexual harassment but also a written guarantee that the department would defend us against his recriminations.

Our conflicts with the department chair and with Untel dragged on. Professing total innocence to some colleagues and reportedly raising the shield of academic freedom to others, Untel further fanned the fires by opposing the proposed departmental code as an invasion of privacy. He also stood by an article he had published in 1975, in which he had boasted that he "lecture[s] to hundreds, and my practiced eye roams freely and fiercely over bosom after bosom . . . rejoicing at beauty, regretting homeliness . . . in both sexes because teaching is a profoundly erotic activity."[26] Now, he reportedly elaborated that the power differential in sexual matters involving students and faculty actually was skewed *toward students*, whom he found superior to professors in beauty and desirability.

Untel's argument was both bizarre and self-incriminating, yet he enjoyed wide support not only among faculty but also among graduate students. Rushing into battle against us, most of our peers smeared us as sluts, feminist plotters, and leftist ideologues out to vilify a conservative professor. Most women graduate students — including those who considered themselves feminists — supported Untel. Some insisted that we must be lying because he had never propositioned *them*, while others argued that Untel was a victim of "partisan divisions," not a perpetrator of harassment.[27] According to individuals who saw her correspondence, one of our peers circulated among some faculty a letter that she had written to the chair to protest our charges against Untel. She cautioned the chair to suspect our motives and to question whether we had invented our allegations just to see the politically conservative Untel squirm.

Despite the adverse political climate in which we pressed our complaints, we secured a measure of relief from the department after two months of struggle. The faculty adopted a code of conduct. Perhaps because several faculty had married either students or one another — or maybe because few faculty could imagine a student who would not happily submit to *their* passes — the code focused on what to do when faculty and students enter romantic relationships rather

26. Source withheld to preserve Untel's anonymity.
27. Source withheld to preserve Untel's anonymity.

than when faculty impose themselves sexually on students. Nevertheless, it was a victory of sorts, for it put harassers on notice that their behavior was unacceptable. We also received a letter of apology from the department which "conclude[d] that there appears to be substantial evidence that improper behavior on the part of Professor [Untel] did take place."[28] The letter went on to apologize for Untel's conduct, to thank us for bringing the problem to light, to pledge "to take every precaution to ensure that this behavior will not be repeated by anyone in the future," and to "do everything in its power to protect [us] from recriminations that might possibly arise from this matter."

A year and a half later, after a campuswide investigation of sexual harassment, the student newspaper published the letter in an account of Untel's conduct and our struggle for redress. Untel's supporters responded with renewed vituperations against us and publicly challenged the legitimacy and validity of the department's letter.[29] Untel himself joined in, denouncing the newspaper story as "McCarthyism."[30] Although he had by now admitted to "verbal improprieties" with the third complainant, Untel again declared himself "innocent of sexual harassment" and reportedly again threatened legal action.[31] In this first big test of its pledge to protect us, the department would not publicly stand by its letter.[32]

At the time of our complaints, no sexual harassment grievance had ever been formally investigated by Cornell University; indeed, no sexual harassment policy had been developed that could guide a grievance process. But by late June 1980 — on the heels of the Untel crisis — university president Frank H. T. Rhodes had issued a statement condemning sexual harassment and urging targets to air their complaints.[33] Still it would be several years before formal procedures would be in place.

I left Cornell for an assistant professorship at the University of

28. George Quester, Chair, letter to complainants, April 25, 1980.
29. Source withheld to preserve Untel's anonymity.
30. Source withheld to preserve Untel's anonymity.
31. Source withheld to preserve Untel's anonymity.
32. Isaac Kramnick to author.
33. Frank H. T. Rhodes memo to Deans, Directors, and Department Heads, "Sexual Harassment," June 20, 1980.

California at Santa Cruz in the fall of 1980. News of my sexual harassment grievance preceded my arrival, so although I escaped the bitterness and rancor that persisted for a time inside the Cornell Government Department, I could not so easily shed the aspersions on my motives or my integrity. Had I left political science I would have been spared the pain that thick academic networks can inflict. But even had I left the academy, I would have taken with me wounds to my spirit that will never completely heal. Doubted — impugned — because of who I was and against whom I complained, I paid for coming forward with my reputation. Smeared by a self-declared jury of my peers — by arrogant and uninformed public opinion — I paid as much for grieving the harassment as I did for the harassment itself. My spirit scarred and my fortitude for personal struggle depleted by events at Cornell University, I took no action at all when a superior in my profession sexually assaulted me a few years later.

SILENCE BROKEN

Although I was oblivious to it, during the winter and spring of 1975 a sexual harassment controversy roiled in Ithaca, New York, where Cornell University is situated and where I lived at the time. Only months before Untel harassed me, Carmita Wood had abruptly quit her job in a Cornell University laboratory, even though she did not have alternative work or income.[34] A mother of four in her mid-forties, Wood had worked in the laboratory for eight years at the time of her unplanned departure in June 1974. Just three years earlier, she had been promoted from the clerical pool to the position of administrative assistant. She was the first woman to reach this status in the laboratory.[35] What prompted her to trade a secure managerial job for an unknown future in an economy troubled by oil shocks, trade imbalances, and stagflation? That's precisely what the unemployment

34. "Women Fight 'Intimidation,'" *Ithaca Journal*, April 5, 1975, 4; Susan Brownmiller and Dolores Alexander, "From Carmita Wood to Anita Hill," *Ms.* (January/February 1992): 70.

35. Lin Farley, *Sexual Shakedown: The Sexual Harassment of Women on the Job* (New York, 1978), quoting Carmita Wood's attorney, Ellen Yackin, 83.

insurance review panel wanted to know six months later when, unable to find another position, Wood applied for benefits. Because she had given up her job voluntarily, Wood's eligibility for benefits depended on whether she had "good cause" for becoming unemployed.[36]

Like so many women before her and since, Carmita Wood did not choose unemployment. She was forced into it. An eminent male scientist she had to deal with at work almost every day subjected her to vulgar and humiliating sexual advances and insinuations. Sometimes he would ogle her from neck to hips, sometimes he would intimate that he was touching himself in her presence, and sometimes he would physically accost her. Once he pinned her against her desk with his body; another time he reached under her sweater and rubbed her skin. Her immediate supervisor was not sympathetic to her distress, and nothing came of her request to move into a different job. Left on her own to fend off the scientist's advances, she developed a painful nerve disorder in her arm and neck, which abated only when the scientist was on leave. Unable to endure the pain and the degradation she anticipated on his return, she quit.[37]

At a hearing to review her claim for unemployment insurance benefits, Wood explained that the scientist's behavior had created "intolerable job conditions."[38] Two co-workers vouched for her description of events: one woman attested to having been harassed herself by the scientist, and Wood's doctor confirmed the adverse effects of job-related stress on her health. There was no question that Wood had been sexually harassed and that she had had to surrender her job because of it. Nonetheless, the unemployment insurance board concluded that quitting had not been her only option and that she must have had other motives for becoming unemployed. Calling her reasons for leaving her job "personal and non-compelling," it de-

36. Diana M. Pearce and Monica L. Phillips, "When Sexual Harassment Happens: State Unemployment Insurance Coverage of Workers Who Leave Their Jobs Because of Sexual Harassment," *Stanford Law and Policy Review*, vol. 5 (Spring 1994): 75.

37. Ellen Yackin, quoted in Farley, *Sexual Shakedown*, 83–84.

38. "Women Fight 'Intimidation.'"

nied her claim.[39] She appealed to the New York State Department of Labor, which turned her down in October 1975.[40]

When Carmita Wood fought back against sexual intimidation at work and then fought to receive unemployment benefits, she entered uncharted legal and political terrain. The law against sex discrimination in employment was barely ten years old in 1974, with core doctrines yet to be decided.[41] Title VII of the Civil Rights Act of 1964 made it an "unlawful employment practice . . . to [hire, fire, limit, segregate, or classify] or otherwise to discriminate against any individual with respect to his [sic] compensation, terms, conditions, or privileges of employment, because of such individual's race, color, religion, sex, or national origin."[42] Despite this strong language, its meaning would require years of litigation and further legislation to be made clear. Does Title VII bar employers from treating pregnant women workers differently from other workers?[43] Does it permit employers ever to exclude all women (or all men) from certain kinds of jobs?[44] Does it require employers to pay women at the same rate

39. Ibid. Some of the details of Carmita Wood's story are drawn from Catharine MacKinnon, *The Sexual Harassment of Working Women* (New Haven, 1979), 42, 78–80.

40. New York State Department of Labor, Unemployment Insurance Appeal Board, Appeal No. 207,958, October 6, 1975.

41. The legal framework for sex discrimination in employment was established in a series of cases spanning the 1970s: see, e.g., *Diaz v. Pan American World Airways, Inc.*, 442 F. 2d. 385, *cert. denied* (5th Cir., 1971); *Dothard v. Rawlinson*, 433 U.S. 321 (1977); *Texas Dept. of Community Affairs v. Burdine*, 450 U.S. 248 (1981).

42. 42 U.S.C. Section 2000e(2)(a)(1) and (2).

43. *General Electric Co. v. Gilbert*, 429 U.S. 125 (1976), established that an employer's disability plan that excluded coverage for pregnancy did not discriminate on the basis of sex because "[t]here is no risk from which men are protected and women are not. Likewise, there is no risk from which women are protected and men are not." According to the Court, pregnancy is an *additional* risk, and its exclusion did not disturb gender parity in the plan's benefits. This decision was effectively vacated when Congress enacted the Pregnancy Discrimination Act in 1978.

44. *Dothard v. Rawlinson* held that a woman could be excluded from employment as a prison guard because she was a woman. In this case sex was accepted as a bona fide occupational qualification because "a woman's relative

as men, if their work is equivalent though their jobs are dissimilar?[45] These kinds of questions monopolized public discussions of sex discrimination in the mid-1970s, as women workers challenged their wholesale segregation and devaluation in the labor force. They remain points of heated contention in courts, unions, and workplaces even today, but they are now part of a larger constellation of discriminatory practices that have come into public view.

That larger constellation includes sexual harassment, which is most typically characterized by the sexualized extortion, intimidation, humiliation, or exploitation of women by men. Although there have been cases of harassment of a man by a woman and of same-sex harassment, harassment is typically heterosexual and directed from man to woman.[46] Sometimes harassment is not sexual but still is clearly based on sex because it is motivated by hostility to the presence of women (or men) in the workplace or at school.[47] My concern in this book is harassment that is sexual: harassment that reduces a woman to her sexuality; that uses sexual acts, propositions, insinuations, or epithets to threaten or shame a woman into suffering subordination; and that chokes a woman's sexual autonomy and agency by subjecting her to unilateral sexual conduct.

A sexual harasser defines a woman by her sex, then deploys sex in ways that interfere with her ability to do her job or get an education. He does this when he demands sex in exchange for advancement, or

---

ability to maintain order in a male, maximum security, unclassified penitentiary . . . could be directly reduced by her womanhood."

45. Courts have generally said no. See, e.g., *Hodgson v. Robert Hall Clothes, Inc.*, 473 F. 2d. 589 (3rd Cir., 1973); *AFSCME v. State of Washington,* 770 F. 2d. 1401 (9th Cir., 1985).

46. The Supreme Court recognized same-sex sexual harassment claims under Title VII in *Oncale v. Sundowner Offshore Services, Inc.*, 523 U.S. 75 (1998).

47. Equal Employment Opportunity Commission, *Policy Guidance on Sexual Harassment,* "Guidance," Part C (4), March 19, 1990, reprinted in Barbara Lindemann and David D. Kadue, *Sexual Harassment in Employment Law* (Washington, D.C., 1992), 672; *McKinney v. Dole,* 765 F. 2d. 1129 (D.C. Cir., 1985); *Hall v. Gus Construction Co.,* 842 F. 2d. 1010 (8th Cir., 1988); *Hicks v. Gates Rubber Co.,* 833 F. 2d. 1406 (10th Cir., 1987); *Oncale v. Sundowner Offshore Services, Inc.*

when he objectifies and sexualizes a woman against her will, or when he infects her work or school environment with sexual taunts and threats to her sexual safety. When he makes sex a condition of employment or education, a harasser forces on a woman unbearable alternatives: comply or lose her job; resist or be harmed; be silent or be shunned. When a harasser so distorts a woman's choices that they are no longer choices at all, he exploits his power over her.

Power always excites the harasser, whether he has formal authority over his prey or craves domination of his peer. Harassers may use power to coerce sex, or they may use sex to exert power. The harm harassment causes intensifies as the formal power differential between a harasser and his target increases. Yet whether a superior or a peer, a harasser abuses power when he makes submission to his unilateral, intrusive, and coercive sexual attention or behavior a condition of his target's ability to do her job, or to earn a fair wage, or to receive an education. Either way, a harasser uses sex to control a woman's status when he threatens his target's dignity, safety, and self-determination. In these ways, harassers enforce women's inequality.

The use of sex as a weapon of inequality has a long history. Across the centuries, enslaved women, factory women, waitresses, and domestic workers have been especially vulnerable to men's sexual impositions. Carmita Wood and other harassed women hoped to change history beginning in 1974 by exposing their harassers and demanding remedies for their injuries. By then they had the law on their side, if only courts would enforce it: in addition to Title VII's ban on sex discrimination in employment, Title IX of the 1972 Education Act Amendments banned sex discrimination in education.[48] By then we also had a vigorous and legally savvy women's movement.

Courts initially resisted women's claims that intimidating sexual conduct discriminates against them based on sex. The first court to receive such a claim threw it out, holding that "the substance of [the]

48. Title IX of the *Education Act Amendments of 1972* provides that "No person in the United States shall, on the basis of sex, be excluded from participation in, be denied the benefits of, or be subjected to discrimination under any education program or activity receiving Federal financial assistance." 20 U.S.C. Section 1681.

complaint is that she was discriminated against, not because she was a woman but because she refused to engage in a sexual affair with her supervisor."[49] In March 1975—just as Carmita Wood was about to go public with her grievance—a second court denied two women the right to relief under the Civil Rights Act, arguing that intimidating sexual conduct is "nothing more than a personal proclivity, peculiarity or mannerism . . . satisfying a personal urge."[50] Declaring it "ludicrous to hold that the sort of activity involved here" constituted sex discrimination, the court reasoned that were it to do so "the only sure way an employer could avoid such charges would be to have employees who were asexual."[51]

Thus did courts in Washington, D.C., and Arizona deny redress to Paulette Barnes, whose job was abolished when she would not have sex with her boss, and to Jane Corne and Geneva DeVane, who were forced by their harasser's conduct to quit their jobs. Likewise, the unemployment review board rejected Carmita Wood's appeal. She did not carry her appeal beyond the state labor department and she never filed a Title VII claim, but her plight triggered a movement to publicize the toll sexual intimidation exacts from women's lives, opportunities, and self-respect with the goal of winning legal remedies for it. This movement gave a name to sexual harassment, put faces on its victims, and brought it out of the closet.

Shortly after a hearing on Carmita Wood's unemployment insurance claim in March 1975, a number of women in Ithaca met to support Wood and to discuss the issues her situation raised. Several members of Working Women United had helped Wood find legal representation for her unemployment insurance appeal. What emerged from the group's conversations about the Wood case was just how common Wood's experience had been. According to one member, "we found many of the women at the meeting had had similarly distasteful experiences—male bosses propositioning women and threatening to fire them if they did not carry through, leering and never looking up beyond a woman's chin when talking with

49. *Barnes v. Train*, 13 FEP Cases 123, 124 (1974 WL 10628 (D.D.C.)).
50. *Corne v. Bausch and Lomb, Inc.*, 390 F. Supp. 161, 163 (D. Ariz., 1975).
51. Ibid., at 164.

them, just making life difficult having to work in the same office."
Cornell instructor Lin Farley explained: "It took women telling the
untold truth about our lives to show how widespread and damaging
these problems really are."[52]

To bring visibility to the problem and to show women who have
been harassed that theirs is not a private shame but a public discrimination, Working Women United convened a speak-out at an Ithaca
community center on May 4, 1975. Karen DeCrow, then-president
of the National Organization for Women, hailed the event: "It's
about time. This is one of the few sexist issues which has been totally
in the closet. . . . As we begin to speak out about such indignities, we
realize that this is not a personal problem, but rather a class problem
which we as females share."[53] The 275 women who attended the
rally in Ithaca listened to 25 women like Carmita Wood talk publicly
about sexual issues despite risk of ridicule and embarrassment in the
wider community.[54] By the summer of 1975, women's accounts of
sexual harassment were heard in New York City, where the city's
Commission on Human Rights held hearings on women and work.
By the fall, the issue had touched a nerve among women nationally
after broad syndication of a *New York Times* report on women's testimony before the commission.[55] By 1976 at least one court had come
to view sexual harassment as a form of sex discrimination.[56]

Carmita Wood's story sounded familiar to many women, for sexual harassment is pervasive: a 1981 government study reported that
84 percent of female federal workers had endured some degree of
verbal or physical sexual imposition; more recent studies estimate

52. "Women Fight 'Intimidation.'"

53. "NOW President Lauds Speak Out," *Ithaca Journal*, May 1, 1975, 6.

54. Karen Lindsey, "Sexual Harassment on the Job and How to Stop It,"
Ms. (November, 1977): 50.

55. Enid Nemy, "Women Begin to Speak Out Against Sexual Harassment at Work," *New York Times*, August 19, 1975, 38. An indication of how
far we've come since 1975: this article originally ran in the "Family/Style"
section of the *Times*.

56. *Williams v. Saxbe et al.*, 413 F. Supp. 654 (D.D.C., 1976), upholding
Diane Williams's cause of action in her case against a male supervisor whose
sexual advances she had rebuffed.

that one of every two women will be harassed either on the job or at school.[57] Despite the prevalence of harassment, many women and men have been slow to grasp that harassment is more than a private or interpersonal matter — that it has public consequences requiring public remediation.

One problem has been that the weapon of the harasser is sex. Most of the time, sex is about desire, pleasure and intimate expression. As such, it is one of the most private aspects of our lives; at least where mutual heterosex between adults is involved, we shield it from public surveillance. Because a harasser's conduct involves sex, it is tempting to excuse that conduct as "just about sex" and therefore walled off in a zone of privacy. The sex in sexual harassment, however, is not mutual, and its private impact has public consequences. Sex is at once a means and an end for the harasser: a means to exert power and an end secured by power (including, sometimes, force). The sex in sexual harassment is an imposition, a cause of harm, a source of inequality; as such, it is never "just about sex" but always about power. It injures never from boorish inadvertence and always from subordinating action.

Another impediment to the public remediation of sexual harassment has been that sexual harassment generally arises from individual conduct. Most of the time, discrimination takes the form of institutional policy or official action, not individual behavior. That an individual's behavior on the job or at school could constitute sex discrimination is not self-evident to many people even today, especially given the privacy we accord most heterosexual conduct short of forcible stranger rape, incest, or child molestation.

Even less accepted has been the legal premise that whether sexualized conduct is sexual harassment depends on how a woman experiences it, not on how a man intends it: "I was just trying to be friendly" is not a defense against verbal or physical sexual injury to a woman. Because sexual harassment is not about what men want but about what women endure, perpetrators often try to rebut claims of injury by impugning the behavior and character of the women they

57. Louise F. Fitzgerald, "Sexual Harassment: Violence Against Women in the Workplace," *American Psychologist* 48 (October 1993): 1071.

harass — as if by their choices or demeanor women invite sexual intrusions and as if it is not the harassers' behavior but women's motives or mental states that cause harm. Some people, like Carmita Wood's male supervisor, have thought that sexual harassment is of women's own making and that they should "try not to get into these situations."[58] Others have wondered whether women exaggerate the effects of oafish flirtation or whether women might contribute to "these situations" themselves. Still others have worried that women trump up offenses just to get back at men they don't particularly like.

If public discussions of Paula Jones's charges against Bill Clinton are any measure, these sorts of concerns still weigh heavily on people's minds. We may now all agree that sexual harassment is sex discrimination. And we may all agree that certain actions, such as a teacher's offering a higher grade to a student who will sleep with him or a supervisor's firing a woman who will not, constitute sexual harassment. But most harassment is not archetypical: sexual extortion is not always explicit; retaliation is not necessarily tangible; fear is not quantifiable; and humiliation is as various as perpetrators and the women they harass. Twenty-five years of litigation and four Supreme Court decisions favorable to women plaintiffs have produced a consensus that sexual harassment is wrong,[59] but they have not produced a consensus about what sexual harassment really is, how to tell when it has happened, whether it warrants punishment, or whether women who complain of it are to be believed.

Since 1980 the Equal Employment Opportunity Commission, the agency that enforces employment rights, has said that if an employer or co-worker subjects an employee to "unwelcome sexual advances, requests for sexual favors, and other verbal or physical conduct of a sexual nature . . . either explicitly or implicitly [as] a term or condition of an individual's employment . . . [or] as the basis for employment decisions . . . [or if] such conduct has the purpose or effect of unreasonably interfering with an individual's work performance or creating an intimidating, hostile, or offensive working environment"

---

58. Ellen Yackin, quoted in Farley, *Sexual Shakedown*, 83.

59. *Meritor Savings Bank v. Vinson*, 477 U.S. 57 (1986); *Harris v. Forklift Systems, Inc.*, 510 U.S. 17 (1993); *Faragher v. City of Boca Raton*; *Burlington Industries, Inc. v. Ellerth*.

that employer or co-worker has committed sexual harassment.[60] In its first sexual harassment decision, the Supreme Court in 1986 endorsed and clarified this definition, explaining that sexual harassment can pose "an arbitrary barrier to sexual equality at the workplace" by polluting the work environment, even if the harm it brings to its target is intangible and psychological rather than tangible and economic.[61] The Court further established that "the gravamen of any sexual harassment claim is that the alleged sexual advances were 'unwelcome,'" not whether the target resisted or acquiesced to them.[62] According to the Court, then, harassment cases do not turn on how a woman responds to her harasser but on whether her harasser impairs the conditions under which she works (or learns).

Still, the Court does distinguish between harassment that makes submission a condition of employment (quid pro quo) and harassment that creates offensive and intimidating employment conditions (hostile environment). Sexual harassment law calibrates the harms of and remedies for unwelcome sexual conduct based on whether its consequences are explicit or implicit, direct or indirect, tangible or intangible. The law treats documented, directly tangible adverse employment consequences stringently, holding employers strictly liable if harassment has occurred. Where harassment's toll is implicit or intangible, the unwelcome sexual conduct must be severe or pervasive to be actionable as sex discrimination. The law thus distinguishes between "simple teasing, offhand comments, and isolated incidents" and discrimination.[63] It does not, however, require a woman to cross a numerical threshold of abuse before she can legitimately complain of her harasser's conduct.[64]

---

60. Equal Employment Opportunity Commission, *Rules and Regulations*, 29 CFR Part 1604, Section 1604.11(a) (November 10, 1980); *Guidelines on Discrimination Because of Sex*, 63 FR 29958, Section 1604.11(a) (current through June 2, 1998).

61. *Meritor Savings Bank v. Vinson*, 66, 68.

62. *Meritor Savings Bank v. Vinson*, 68, 64, 66.

63. *Faragher v. City of Boca Raton*, at 788; *Oncale v. Sundowner Offshore Services, Inc.*, at 82.

64. Ibid., at 8, "expressing no opinion as to whether a single unfulfilled threat is sufficient to constitute discrimination in the terms or conditions of employment."

Both judges and the public have accepted the Supreme Court's framework for assessing sexual harassment, at least as a theoretical matter, but both lower courts and the public have expressed reservations about the framework as a legal application and have contrived tough standards for actionable harassment, such as requiring that it must be repeated, extreme, and tangibly harmful. Almost everyone agrees that sexual harassment is wrong; the difficulty is in deciding whether a particular complainant has been harassed. Lower court judges and the public have been most resistant to the concept of hostile environment sexual harassment, the kind of harassment that depends on how a man's unwelcome sexual conduct made a woman feel rather than on objective measures of his conduct and its consequences.

Following the law established by the Supreme Court, a hostile environment complainant needs to persuade a fact finder that her perpetrator's conduct was unwanted and that it offended, humiliated, or frightened her such that it perverted the environment in which she was to learn or to do her job. The Supreme Court has not required her to prove that the offensive conduct occurred more than once, that her harasser did not heed her rebuff, or that he caused her economic harm. Hostile environment sexual harassment turns on a woman's subjective experience, and ultimately, on a judge's or jury's understanding of that experience as severely or pervasively offensive.

Some judges have deflated the significance of a woman's experience in hostile environment cases by inventing new thresholds for harm or by squeezing hostile environment issues into the quid pro quo framework. Ruling for defendant Bill Clinton's motion for summary judgment in *Jones v. Clinton*, for example, Judge Susan Webber Wright argued that a superior who told a woman to kiss his exposed penis, then fondled himself when she did not, may be "boorish and offensive" but is not a harasser because he abandoned his request "as soon as the plaintiff made clear that the advance was not welcome."[65] Holding Paula Jones to the definition of quid pro quo harassment in

65. "Memorandum Opinion and Order," *Jones v. Clinton*, 1998 WL 148370, 15, 17 (E.D. Ark., 1998), holding that even if what Paula Jones alleged were true, she had no cause for legal action.

making her hostile environment claim, Wright further maintained that the lack of "any materially significant disadvantage . . . dispel[s] the notion that [the complainant] was subjected to a hostile work environment."[66] At least one leading feminist agreed with the judge, describing the alleged harassment as "a clumsy sexual pass"[67] that happened only once and characterizing the complainant's claim as "borderline" because it lacked "demonstrable job consequences."[68]

If the law and the people understand sexual harassment differently, they also differ on how rigorously the law should police harassing behavior. Title VII of the Civil Rights Act prohibits all discrimination on the basis of sex, race, religion, or nativity. A pivotal question in civil rights law is when practices that adversely affect women (or men) do so "because of sex" rather than because of some other factor not precluded by law. Once a practice such as sexual harassment is determined to discriminate based on sex, it is against the law and must be remedied. Yet, even Anita Hill, whose own account of sexual harassment riveted the country, allowed that we might want to put President Clinton's alleged sexual harassment into a larger context — to weigh his alleged discrimination against individual women against the fact that he was elected in spite of it and against his policy record on women's issues.[69]

As we see in the next chapter, subjective and imprecise language in the law of sexual harassment has permitted some courts to protect harassers or to limit remedies available to victims. Nevertheless, the core elements of sexual harassment law have developed ineluctably, if haltingly, toward improving women's prospects for securing jus-

66. "Memorandum Opinion and Order," *Jones v. Clinton*, at 14.

67. Gloria Steinem, "Feminists and the Clinton Question," *New York Times*, March 22, 1998.

68. Gloria Steinem on National Public Radio, "Women React to Jones Dismissal," *Morning Edition*, April 2, 1998.

69. Anita Hill, interview with Tim Russert, *Meet the Press*, March 22, 1998: "we have to look at the totality of the presidency and how has he been on women's issues generally. Is he our best bet, notwithstanding some behavior that we might dislike? And I don't think that most women have come to the point where we've said, 'Well, this is so bad that even if he is better on the bigger issues, we can't have him as president.'" (Burrelle's Transcripts, p. 14).

tice.[70] In contrast, public attitudes toward the law have been ambivalent, and sometimes downright hostile. Some hostility is to be expected because sexual harassment law disturbs old habits, checks power, and constrains self-gratification that risks harm to others. To some conservatives, such restraint on behavior asphyxiates liberty. Justice Clarence Thomas, for example, has complained that strengthened standards for employer liability in harassment cases are "incompatible with a free society,"[71] while the *New Republic* has warned that "this means adopting something close to a zero-tolerance policy for sexual expression . . . free expression more generally will suffer."[72]

More remarkably, ambivalence toward the law has now spread to some of the law's earliest and staunchest proponents—Democratic women and feminists. Gloria Steinem, for example, would shield a superior's first request for oral sex from legal reproach as long as he accepts rejection.[73] Meanwhile, with support from 90 percent of its 500 chapters, the National Organization for Women declined to contribute a friend-of-the-court brief on behalf of Paula Jones's appeal of Judge Wright's summary judgment against her, even though the judge had distorted the hostile environment framework to a plaintiff's disadvantage. NOW president Patricia Ireland called Jones's "an imperfect case" advanced by "disreputable" characters.[74]

The idea that there are perfect cases and that perfect cases are the ones we should support burdens most women who seek redress for sexual harassment. Most harassment involves complexities of one sort or another, especially when there are no witnesses or when the intimidation or extortion is subtle or implicit. Most reported harassment involves targets who can no longer tolerate their harassers.

70. *Gebser v. Lago Vista Independent School District*, 524 U.S. 274, is a significant exception, discussed in note 76, below.

71. *Burlington Industries, Inc. v. Ellerth*, Justice Thomas dissenting, at 51.

72. "Anti-Expressionism," *The New Republic* (July 20 and 27, 1998): 8.

73. Steinem, "Feminists and the Clinton Question"; Steinem on National Public Radio, *Morning Edition*, April 2, 1998.

74. Washington Transcript Service, "Patricia Ireland Director, National Organization for Women Holds News Conference to Launch Emergency Initiative to Stop Sexual Harassment," April 22, 1998; Interview with Patricia Ireland, *This Week with Sam Donaldson and Cokie Roberts*, ABC Transcript #861, April 26, 1998.

Moreover, all harassment begins with a single incident. If we follow Steinem, a woman who cannot show us tangible injuries or who reported her harassment the first time it happened may not have a right to her day in court. If we follow Ireland, a woman whose legal claim is not ironclad or whose supporters are hostile to feminism may not have a case even in the court of feminist opinion.

Misgivings about the meaning and measure of sexual harassment in part reflect genuine confusion about how to balance one person's liberty against another's right to equal opportunity. They also express qualms about the fairness of a process that turns on a woman's subjective response to a man's objective behavior. These concerns mount and subside depending on our view of individual women who complain of harassment. Is she loose? Is she thin-skinned? Is she a prude? Does she have an ax to grind? Often, our concerns also depend on our feelings about the alleged harasser. Do we like him? Does he have clout? Has he been good to us? As the director of New York State's Unemployment Insurance Division said during Carmita Wood's appeal, sexual harassment can be "good cause for leaving a job. If true, we would pay benefits without question. But it's one of the toughest cases to handle. It's a question of credibility."[75]

PRECARIOUS POLITICS

Carmita Wood and the speak-out she inspired began a process of legal change that has produced both safeguards and redress for women (and men) who have been sexually harassed. Although sexual harassment law is stronger in employment than in education,[76] in both venues sexual harassment is a prohibited form of sex discrimination and its targets can expect institutions to enforce that prohibition. The law contains limits and contradictions, however, as we might ex-

75. Enid Nemy, "Women Begin to Speak Out Against Sexual Harassment at Work."

76. *Gebser v. Lago Vista Independent School District* established that because Congress did not explictly state an agency theory of discrimination in Title IX, school districts cannot be held liable for sexual harassment by individual faculty unless an official with the authority to effect policy had actual knowledge of the harassment and was "deliberately indifferent" to it.

pect of any law that disturbs gender, race, or class prerogatives. Imperfect cases brought by imperfect women often are swallowed by the law's loopholes, disappointing many women who seek the law's remedies and disarming others before their harassers. Still, if the law of sexual harassment is itself imperfect, it nevertheless asserts the crucial principle that violations of women's sexual autonomy, safety, and self-respect are offenses against equality.

Pathbreaking work by Catharine MacKinnon, the Women's Legal Defense Fund, the National Women's Law Center, and the NOW Legal Defense and Education Fund has made discrimination law responsive to inequality as women experience it. The responsiveness of discrimination law to sexualized inequality hangs on its premise: that it is the effects of a perpetrator's sexualized action on his target that matter. To be sure, the standards by which we assess the effects of harassment can impede a claimant's satisfaction. For example, under the "reasonable person" standard that judges and juries use to test sexual harassment allegations, a plaintiff's complaint against a man's abusive sexual conduct might be dismissed as her own "hypersensitive overreaction" to ordinary sexual horseplay. Yet, even as the law requires women to show that their reactions to harassment are reasonable, it also requires judges and juries to examine women's experiences of unwelcomed sexualization as if women's experiences have a bearing on our equality.

The law is stronger than the individuals who live under it, but only as long as they agree to it. When people misapprehend or resent the law, as it seems many do sexual harassment law, we run the risk that their representatives will erode or overturn it. The risk is compounded when people distrust those who use the law, as they do women who allege sexual harassment. People do rebel against laws they don't like, and politicians do defer to public opinion. Thus is affirmative action under fire, thus was welfare repealed, and thus was the Clinton presidency preserved.

The great irony of 1998 was that just as journalists, legal pundits, Democrats, and feminists struck at the foundation of sexual harassment law in their public commentaries about Paula Jones, Monica Lewinsky, Kathleen Willey, and Bill Clinton, the conservative Supreme Court actually shored it up. Although liberals disdained Paula

Jones's claim because she could not show a "demonstrable job conse-quence," the Court ruled in two cases that employers are liable for sexual harassment by supervisors, whether or not targets suffer tan-gible job-related losses from the harassment.[77]

Given the freshness of these decisions, it is unlikely that sexual harassment law will soon unravel at the hands of the Supreme Court, but it could unravel at the hands of lower courts. Every day lower courts exercise discretion over questions the Supreme Court has not yet settled definitively. Can a single incident constitute sexual ha-rassment? How severe does it have to be? Must it be felonious as-sault, as Judge Wright implied when she granted Bill Clinton's mo-tion to dismiss Paula Jones's claim?[78] Judges' answers to these sorts of questions can open sexual harassment law to more women, or they can close the law to all but the most extreme cases.

Likewise, Congress, with its power to amend Title VII, can ad-vance or reverse sexual harassment safeguards and remedies. Increas-ingly articulate public aversion to how the law works could well arouse Congress to constrain it. For example, Congress could im-pose a numerical threshold for harassment; it could reduce the mon-etary damages available to successful sexual harassment plaintiffs; it could hold losing complainants liable for legal expenses; it could sur-round alleged harassers with a privacy shield against inquiries into patterns of sexually harassing conduct; it could even redefine sex dis-crimination to exclude sexual matters.[79]

More worrisome than political fallout on the law itself, however, is the fallout on women who need to use it. The law is only as impor-tant as its effect on people's lives. Unless women can be confident that harassment always should be reported — that their harassment counts no matter how imperfect their circumstances — the law will

77. *Faragher v. City of Boca Raton; Burlington Industries, Inc. v. Ellerth.*

78. "Memorandum Opinion and Order," *Jones v. Clinton,* at 15.

79. See, e.g., Robert J. Samuelson, "All Because of a Defective Law," *Wash-ington Post,* August 12, 1998, calling on Congress to legislate limits to sexual harassment law; see also, Steven Brill, "Paula Jones: There Ought to Be a Law," *Washington Post,* June 5, 1994, calling for a legal rule requiring losers to pay winner's legal fees as a way of preventing sexual harassment claims such as Paula Jones's.

fall into disuse among women who most need it: women who are compelled to take jobs in exchange for welfare; women who cannot quit their jobs because they are poor; women for whom work will never pay if they must survive a gauntlet of sexual abuse or grant requests for sexual favors in order to earn a living.

t w o Sexual Harassment Law from Carmita Wood to Paula Jones

One sign of the hostile political environment inhabited by sexually harassed women is the almost allergic reaction of many men (and some women) to the idea that women's civil rights might require limitations on men's sexual conduct. Especially on the right, critics have despaired that such limitations abrogate men's due process protections and stifle their speech.[1] In the mainstream media, social and legal commenta-

1. See, e.g., Michael S. Greve, "Sexual Harassment: Telling the Other Victims' Story," *Northern Kentucky Law Review* 23 (1996): 523–541; Eugene Volokh, "Freedom of Speech and Workplace Harassment," *UCLA Law Review* 39 (1992): 1791ff.

tors have worried that the regulation of sexual conduct in the work-place leads to unreasonable interference with personal relationships because it blurs the distinction between consensual sex and discrimination.[2] The idea that sexual harassment law restricts normal human expression carries over into popular complaints that the law makes it dangerous for a man to flirt with a woman, to pay her a compliment, to look at her for more than five seconds, or to ask her out. Blaming Bill Clinton's troubles with Paula Jones, Monica Lewinsky, and Kenneth Starr on "the large defects of sexual harassment law," one analyst has charged that "the law makes almost any kind of unwanted sexual speech or conduct potentially illegal if, somehow, it's tied to the workplace [or school]. . . . It suppress[es] men's and women's freedom to deal naturally with each other."[3] Even my feminist father has wondered whether sexual harassment law doesn't expose men who take ordinary romantic or sexual initiative to absurd legal risks.

The policies and practices of some employers and educators have confirmed these concerns, sowing antagonism toward the law by their exaggerated enforcement of it. CNN reported, for example, that some employers are experimenting with dating contracts to prevent soured romantic relationships among employees from giving rise to sexual harassment claims.[4] The Miller Brewing Company fired one of its managers because he discussed the rhymes-with-Dolores *Seinfeld* episode with a female co-worker who didn't want to hear about it.[5] Meanwhile, I've heard progressive male professors forswear ever meeting with a woman student behind closed doors no matter how private the academic or personal problem she wishes to discuss. These sorts of approaches to sexual harassment, however well intended, caricature the problem. Employers' dating contracts,

2. See, e.g., Jeffrey Toobin, "The Trouble With Sex," *The New Yorker* (February 1998): 48–55; Philip Weiss, "Don't Even Think About It (The Cupid Cops Are Watching)," *New York Times Magazine*, May 3, 1998, 42–47, 58–60, 68, 81.

3. Robert J. Samuelson, "All Because of a Defective Law," *Washington Post*, August 12, 1998.

4. CNN, *Newsstand*, August 5, 1998, 7pm PDT.

5. Jennifer Laabs, "Executive Is Found Not Guilty of Sexual Harassment after 'Seinfeld' Episode," *Workforce*, 76 (September 1997): 23.

their sometimes disproportionate responses to sexual harassment complaints, and professors' open-door policies stoke the impression that sexual harassment law requires employers and schools to protect women and men from routine interactions with one another, even at the risk of disturbing the ordinary course of professional and educational duties and even at the price of expressive freedom and personal privacy. What's more, they treat women as if we are all walking sexual harassment time bombs, set to fire charges against whichever man gives us the slightest opportunity.

Today's hyperbolic responses to sexual harassment law echo early judicial resistance to finding sex discrimination in sexual (mis)conduct. When first presented with the issue in the mid-1970s, courts were reluctant to allow women to state a claim under Title VII of the Civil Rights Act if the problem that aggrieved them was a man's sexual conduct. Repeatedly defining sex as personal, even when it injured women's public role, courts generally distinguished between "inexcusable conduct" and "arbitrary [sex-based] barrier[s] to continued employment."[6] Translating the sexual conduct women complained about into natural expressions of men's sexual desire, courts equated prohibitions on sexual harassment with prohibitions on (hetero)sexuality. Further, in the first sexual harassment cases, courts drew a line between discrimination "because she was a woman"— which is prohibited by Title VII—and discrimination "because she refused to engage in a sexual affair with her supervisor"—which courts held beyond the scope of Title VII.[7] These initial judicial reservations toward finding discrimination where conduct is sexual presaged later political opposition to the law the courts eventually designed. Common to the political opposition is the view that what we call sexual harassment is mostly just about sex—idiosyncratic, isolated, and interpersonal, even if sometimes inappropriate.

Beginning in 1974, courts struggled with women's claims to win relief from sexual harassment as a matter of civil rights. By 1980, several appeals courts recognized a connection between sexual conduct

6. *Barnes v. Train*, 13 FEP Cases 123 (D.D.C., 1974) (1974 WL 10628 (D.D.C.)).

7. Ibid.; see also, *Tomkins v. Public Service Electric & Gas Co.*, 422 F. Supp. 553, 556 (D.N.J., 1976).

and discrimination, when that conduct was perpetrated by a supervisor or higher authority *and* when that conduct (or its rebuff) caused measurable economic harm to its target.[8] In 1980, the Equal Employment Opportunity Commission (EEOC) widened the field of sexual conduct to be governed by sex discrimination law. It defined the circumstances and behaviors that constitute sexual harassment to include not only unwelcome sexual advances or practices that result in concrete job disadvantages for the target — denial of a promotion, demotion, or loss of employment — but also those that make it more difficult for a target to do her job. During the early 1980s, courts followed the EEOC to broaden their own frameworks for assessing harassment,[9] and in 1986 the Supreme Court weighed in to confirm that both sexual extortion (quid pro quo) and sexual intimidation (hostile environment) are prohibited forms of sex discrimination.[10]

These legal advances were not definitive, however. As we shall see, a host of collateral issues have preoccupied lower courts ever since the Supreme Court's 1986 ruling in *Meritor Savings Bank v. Vinson*. Although hostile environment theory became a fixture of sexual harassment jurisprudence with *Meritor*, some lower courts subjected plaintiffs to stringent tests under the theory. Linguistic loopholes in the *Meritor* decision itself permitted lower courts to withhold remedies from women who could not demonstrate astounding tangible injuries, even though their economic opportunity had been no less compromised by demeaning, intrusive, or threatening sexual acts or pressures. The Supreme Court closed some of these loopholes during the 1990s, in decisions that strengthened sexual harassment law by recognizing that unwelcome sexual conduct is in itself a discriminatory burden, whether or not it costs a woman her job or physical safety or soaring psychiatric bills.[11] Many key issues

8. *Barnes v. Costle*, 561 F. 2d. 983 (D.C. Cir., 1977); *Tomkins v. Public Service Electric & Gas Co.*, 568 F. 2d. 1044 (3rd Cir., 1977); *Miller v. Bank of America*, 600 F. 2d. 1211 (9th Cir., 1979).

9. The pivotal cases were *Bundy v. Jackson*, 641 F. 2d. 934 (D.C. Cir., 1981) and *Henson v. City of Dundee*, 682 F. 2d. 897 (11th Cir., 1982).

10. *Meritor Savings Bank v. Vinson*, 477 U.S. 57 (1986).

11. *Harris v. Forklift Systems, Inc.*, 510 U.S. 17 (1993); *Faragher v. City of Boca Raton*, 524 U.S. 775 (1998); *Burlington Industries, Inc. v. Ellerth*, 524 U.S. 742 (1998).

await resolution in future litigation, however. For example, are there First Amendment limitations on what sexual harassment law may prohibit? Is there an objective way to measure the injuries caused by sexual conduct if the conduct does not result in palpable harm? Under what circumstances may a target seek redress after a first (or single) incident of extortionate or intimidating sexual conduct?

The Supreme Court has thus far avoided these questions, and lower courts have offered conflicting answers. Limitations, silences, and contradictions in the law inflame political struggles in workplaces and schools, as well as in public debate, over just how far the law should go to defend women against sexualized discrimination. Oddly, the most popular criticism of sexual harassment law is not that it is too weak to relieve the millions of women who have endured sexual extortion or intimidation, let alone to prevent such unwelcome conduct altogether. Rather, it is that the law is so firm, so aggressive, and so chilling that schools and workplaces have become virtual police states with bosses and administrators given carte blanche not only as workplace censors but also as after-hours bedroom snoops. Although courts devised sexual harassment law to remedy flagrantly abusive or extortionate sexual practices in the workplace, politicians and commentators of all stripes, including some feminists, complain that the law stifles expression, invades privacy, denies women's agency, or is just plain antisex.[12] Some male workers, meanwhile, say sexual harassment law makes them fear customary human interaction with women workers — "she might take it the wrong way and I'll be fired." To avoid discriminating against women by sexualizing them, some men now discriminate by ignoring them — by excluding

12. One line of criticism that has enjoyed growing currency is that there's too much sex in sexual harassment law. See, e.g., Toobin, "The Trouble with Sex," *The New Yorker;* Henry Louis Gates, Jr., "Men Behaving Badly: Who Put the Sex in Sexual Harassment?" *The New Yorker* (August 18, 1997): 4–5. Toobin and Gates both make the point that much discriminatory harassment is missed by the focus on sexualized harassment. Toobin borrows from Vicki Schultz, "Reconceptualizing Sexual Harassment," *Yale Law Journal* 107 (1998): 1683–1805. For a presentation of sexual harassment as part of the politics of sex scandal, see Henry Louis Gates, Jr., "The Naked Republic," *The New Yorker* (August 25, 1997): 114–123.

them from mentoring relationships, occupational networks, or business travel.[13]

Sexual harassment law provides women a defense against (or a remedy for) sexual imposition and intimidation in certain institutional settings — workplaces and schools. Why does the idea that unilateral sexual conduct — either to coerce sex or to humiliate with sex — offends equality provoke such resentment and controversy? Part of the reason is that sexual harassment law *is* about sex: in the name of civil rights it sets limits on the sexual prerogatives of gender power. Although in practice the law reaches only egregious conduct, in theory it links women's sexual agency to our independent personhood, thereby calling a continuum of masculine sexual prerogatives into question. Another part of the reason is that the law is *for women.* Its remedies may be available to men as well as to women, but the law arose from women's experiences and established women's legal claim to sexual agency in a gender hierarchy premised on our subordination. Precisely because sexual harassment law is about sex and for women, courts were slow to announce it.

FINDING DISCRIMINATION IN SEXUAL CONDUCT

Paulette Barnes, an African American employee of the Environmental Protection Agency, took the first reported sexual harassment case to court in 1974. Barnes alleged that her supervisor had propositioned her to begin an affair, telling her repeatedly that she would improve her employment status by going along. When she would not, he retaliated first by reassigning her and then by abolishing her job. The case lumbered through processes required by Title VII, which, because Barnes was a government worker, included a review by the Civil Service Commission. When the commission concluded that Title VII did not reach the situation Barnes described, she turned to the courts. In August 1974, the district court granted summary judgment against her, arguing that "this is a personal controversy underpinned by the subtleties of an inharmonious personal relationship."[14] Moreover, the court maintained, the discrimination

13. Susan M. Bentonn-Powers, "Sex Harassment Laws Create New Barriers," *National Law Journal* (June 26, 1995).

14. *Barnes v. Train*, at 123.

Barnes complained of was not based on *sex*—not "because she was a woman"—but based on *sexual* matters—because she declined an affair.[15]

A few months later, a court in Arizona heard a claim filed by Jane Corne and Geneva DeVane against Bausch and Lomb. Following Title VII's requirement that targets of discrimination take their grievances first to the EEOC, Corne and DeVane had secured a notice of the right to sue under Title VII. Their complaint alleged that they had had to quit their jobs as clerical workers because verbal and physical sexual advances from their supervisor created "increasingly onerous" working conditions.[16] The court ruled that even if the conduct Corne and DeVane described had really happened, Title VII could not recognize that conduct as discrimination. Insisting that the case law limited Title VII's purview to discriminatory conduct arising from company policies, not individual action, the court ruled that Title VII guards against discrimination by employers, not against "personal proclivit[ies]" of employees.[17] The court continued, explaining that if such individual actions were actionable under civil rights law, there "would be a potential federal lawsuit every time any employee made amorous or sexually oriented advances toward another."[18]

In 1976, two more courts repeated the argument that if conduct is sexual, it's not based on sex—and therefore it's not discrimination.[19] At the heart of this argument ran three assumptions: first, that sexual matters are private, relational, communicative, and about desire; second, that sexual matters involve both genders; and third, that Title VII governs employment practices, not personal ones. Title VII works to promote workplace opportunity only when employers (or other parties designated by the law, such as unions) can be held responsible for the discrimination that occurs on their watch. If *sexual* discrimination is merely personal—not to mention genderless— then employers cannot be required to remedy it. If there is no rem-

15. Ibid.

16. *Corne v. Bausch and Lomb, Inc.*, 390 F. Supp. 161, 162 (D. Ariz., 1975).

17. Ibid., at 163.

18. Ibid.

19. *Miller v. Bank of America*, 418 F. Supp. 233 (N.D. Calif., 1976); *Tomkins v. Public Service Electric & Gas Co.* (1976).

edy for sexual discrimination, then women do not have a Title VII right to a workplace free of it.

These issues arose in the 1976 case brought by Margaret Miller against the Bank of America. According to Miller, she had been fired after she refused her supervisor's request for sexual favors from a "black chick."[20] She initially filed a race discrimination claim under 42 U.S.C. Section 1981, which prohibits race discrimination in the formation and duration of private contracts, along with both race and sex discrimination claims under Title VII.[21] At the hearing on the bank's motion for summary judgment, Miller conceded that her case stood or fell on the issue of sex discrimination: although Miller's supervisor had racialized his sexual request, he would not have made the request were she not a woman. In granting the bank's motion, the district court accordingly confined itself to Miller's claim that her supervisor's sexual conduct violated Title VII. Echoing *Barnes* and *Corne*, the court defined the supervisor's sexual conduct and subsequent reprisal as "isolated and unauthorized sex misconduct" that Title VII never was intended to regulate. The court further reasoned that because the bank officially opposed sexual misconduct and had an internal grievance procedure that Miller had not used, it was not responsible for the problems Miller faced. If the bank bore no responsibility, then no Title VII remedy was available for Miller, as the statute guaranteed rights not against people but against employment institutions.

Embellishing on *Corne*, the court continued: "In addition . . . it is conceivable, under plaintiff's theory, that flirtations of the smallest order would give rise to liability. The attraction of males to females and females to males is a natural sex phenomenon and it is probable that this attraction plays at least a subtle part in most personnel decisions. Such being the case, it would seem wise for the Courts to refrain from delving into these matters short of specific factual allegations describing an employer policy which in its application imposes

20. *Miller v. Bank of America* (rev'd, 1979).

21. Section 1981 dates to the Civil Rights Act of 1866. Because it permits monetary remedies beyond the equitable relief to which Title VII was limited until 1991, race discrimination cases often have been litigated under both provisions.

or permits a consistent, as distinguished from isolated, sex-based discrimination."[22] Unable to see either abuses of power or systemic inequalities in Miller's supervisor's conduct, the *Miller* court reduced sexual extortion to a mundane social interaction. Following *Barnes* and *Corne*, *Miller* drew a sharp boundary around sex discrimination law, effectively excluding the most personal and disempowering violations of women's economic personhood from legal scrutiny.

Women who had been asked to trade sex for employment were dealt a fourth blow late in 1976, when a district court in New Jersey embraced the logic of *Barnes*, *Corne*, and *Miller*. Adrienne Tomkins sued her employer, Public Service Electric and Gas Company, charging that she had been fired because she had rebuffed her supervisor's sexual advances.[23] In line for a promotion to a secretarial position, she had accepted her supervisor's request that they lunch together at a nearby restaurant, ostensibly to discuss her situation. At lunch, he made sexual overtures toward her, indicated he wanted to have sex with her, and told her that she needed to comply if they were to have a satisfactory working relationship.[24] She complained to company officials, expressing her intention to quit because of the incident. She was offered a transfer, but was placed in a lower-level position where she received negative evaluations and threats of demotion. Ultimately, the company fired her. Tomkins's legal claim asserted that her supervisor's proposition constituted a discriminatory "term and condition" of employment and that the company's retaliatory employment decisions amounted to sex-based preferential treatment of her supervisor and discrimination against her.

While the court held that Tomkins did raise a Title VII issue with her preferential treatment claim, it dismissed her discrimination charge against the sexual conduct of her supervisor. Reiterating the basic argument of *Barnes*, *Corne*, and *Miller*— only more starkly — the court declared: "Title VII was enacted in order to remove those artificial barriers to full employment which are based upon unjust and long-encrusted prejudice. . . . It is not intended to provide a fed-

22. *Miller v. Bank of America*, at 236 (1976).
23. *Tomkins v. Public Service Electric & Gas Co.* (1976).
24. Restatement of facts, *Tomkins v. Public Service Electric & Gas Co.* (rev'd 1977).

eral tort remedy for what amounts to physical attack motivated by sexual desire on the part of a supervisor and which happened to occur in a corporate corridor rather than a back alley." Besides distinguishing between remedies in criminal law and remedies against sex discrimination, the court also maintained that a woman's sex has nothing to do with a male supervisor's unwelcome conduct, "even when the purpose is sexual."[25]

Unlike the *Barnes*, *Corne*, and *Miller* courts, the *Tomkins* court did recognize that the harm to Adrienne Tomkins sprang from her supervisor's power over her. However, the court explained, the abuse of power is not intrinsically sexual and is not drawn along gender lines: "The abuse of authority by supervisors of either sex for personal purposes is an unhappy and recurrent feature of our social experience."[26] Arguing that sexual submission is not a gender-specific criterion — that abusive sexual conduct could be directed by a woman against a man — the court concluded that sexual submission could not be sex discrimination even when demanded only of women (or only of men). The court further reasoned that if a supervisor's unrequited expression of sexual desire was deemed to discriminate "because of sex," "the floodgates to litigation" would be opened: "If the plaintiff's view were to prevail, no superior could, prudently, attempt to open a social dialogue with any subordinate of either sex. An invitation to dinner could become an invitation to a federal lawsuit if a once harmonious relationship turned to sour at some later time. And if an inebriated approach by a supervisor to a subordinate at the office Christmas party could form the basis of a federal lawsuit for sex discrimination if a promotion or a raise is later denied to the subordinate, we would need 4,000 federal trial judges instead of some 400."[27]

The obtuseness of the *Barnes*, *Corne*, *Miller*, and *Tomkins* courts seemed to suggest that Title VII was a dead end for sexually harassed women workers. However, in April 1976 — after *Barnes* and *Corne* but before *Miller* and *Tomkins* — a federal district court in Washington, D.C., bucked the trend, issuing the first judicial ruling in favor

25. *Tomkins v. Public Service Electric & Gas Co.*, at 556 (1976).
26. Ibid., at 557.
27. Ibid.

of a sexual harassment plaintiff. The D.C. court agreed with Diane Williams that when her supervisor humiliated, threatened, and ultimately fired her following her rejection of his sexual advances, he discriminated against her based on sex. In reaching this conclusion, the court expounded an analysis that would soon draw sexual extortion by supervisors under the jurisdiction of Title VII.[28]

The *Williams* court concerned itself with two questions: first, whether "willingness to furnish sexual consideration"[29] was a sex-based employment criterion; and second, whether retaliation by a rebuffed supervisor was "an isolated personal incident"[30] or an employment action. Citing the settled judicial view that "Congress intended to strike at the entire spectrum of disparate treatment of men and women resulting from sex stereotypes,"[31] the *Williams* court struggled to place sexual harassment on that spectrum. It had to dispense with two kinds of arguments to do so: one was that sex had to be the sole basis for the discrimination; the other was that the discrimination had to be based on a characteristic peculiar to one of the sexes. On the first point, the court held that if a practice or a rule is applied only to one sex, then sex discrimination has occurred — even if the practice or rule is conceptually sex-neutral. The court built this conclusion from Title VII precedents striking down marriage bars for female flight attendants (both sexes marry) and restricted employment for mothers of young children (both sexes are parents).[32] Following this reasoning, even though both women and men have sex, the fact that sexual favors were demanded of women and not men (or vice versa) turned sexual extortion into sex discrimination.

The court spent less time on the second point, ruling that whether Williams's supervisor's retaliatory actions are indeed "isolated" and "personal" is a factual question to be sorted out in a hearing or trial.

28. *Williams v. Saxbe*, 413 F. Supp. 654 (D.D.C., 1976).

29. Ibid., at 658.

30. Ibid., at 660.

31. *Sprogis v. United Air Lines, Inc.*, 444 F. 2d. 1194, 1198 (7th Cir., 1971).

32. Ibid.; *Phillips v. Martin Marietta Corp.*, 400 U.S. 542 (1971) (upholding the 5th Circuit's analysis that a policy that allowed men with preschool children to be hired into certain positions, but that prohibited women with preschool children from the same positions, was sex discrimination.)

This of course established Williams's standing to establish the facts. Further, the court maintained that the supervisor's actions might well have implicated employment policies or practices, even if the employer did not officially condone such actions. Borrowing from common law rules of *respondeat superior*, the court explained that the supervisor is an agent of the employer. When a supervisor uses job benefits or detriments to extort sex from a subordinate, he is trading on the power conferred to him by his employer. According to this view, liability for the sexualized abuse of power by supervisors ultimately rests with the employer. As a practice related to employment for which the employer is responsible, sexual extortion thus falls under the purview of Title VII.

The *Williams* decision foreshadowed a torpid judicial shift toward extending Title VII remedies to targets of sexual harassment. Barnes, Corne and DeVane, Tomkins, and Miller all appealed the district court judgments against them. On appeal, each won the right to claim redress under Title VII for the sexual extortion each had endured. The *Barnes* and *Tomkins* appellate decisions were pivotal, setting precedents in reasoning and outcome against which cumbersome collateral issues in *Corne* and *Miller* would be weighed.[33] Notably, *Barnes* and *Tomkins* were influenced by feminist legal advocates — Catharine MacKinnon, in *Barnes*, and Nadine Taub, of the Women's Rights Litigation Clinic, as counsel in *Tomkins*, with Equal Rights Advocates as *amicus*.[34]

Tackling the riddle of whether sexual requests are sex-based — and thus whether retaliation for unrequited sex is discrimination — the *Barnes* appeals court determined that "[b]ut for her womanhood, from aught that appears, her participation in sexual activity would never have been solicited. . . . [S]he became the target of her supe-

33. *Barnes v. Costle* (1977); *Tomkins v. Public Service Electric & Gas Co.* (1977); *Corne v. Bausch and Lomb, Inc.*, 562 F. 2d. 55 (9th Cir., 1977); *Corne v. Bausch and Lomb, Inc.*, 1978 WL 205, 1 (D. Ariz., 1978); *Miller v. Bank of America* (1979).

34. MacKinnon reportedly supplied a copy of a paper she had written on sexual harassment to a law clerk assigned to the *Barnes* case in the appeals court. Her father, conservative Judge George MacKinnon, was one of the judges who heard the case. See Toobin, "The Trouble with Sex," *The New Yorker*.

rior's sexual desires because she was a woman, and was asked to bow to his demands as the price for holding her job."[35] Key to the court's assertion that Barnes had been subjected to sexual requests because she was a woman was its finding that "no male employee was susceptible to such an approach by appellant's supervisor."[36] According to the court, the only circumstance under which the supervisor's conduct would have been sexual but not sex-based was if he had extorted sex from both women and men.[37]

Applying its logic to the detrimental employment decisions taken against Barnes by her supervisor, the court rebutted the district court's notion that Barnes's termination was not sex-based discrimination, but was the consequence of her refusal to comply sexually. Reviewing a long line of Title VII cases outside the sexual harassment context, the court found that sex discrimination occurs even when a person's sex is not the only basis for an adverse action. Although Paulette Barnes was fired because she rejected her supervisor's sexual advances, not simply because she was a woman, "but for" the fact that she was a woman, she would not have received those advances in the first place.[38]

In November 1977, the Third Circuit heard Adrienne Tomkins's appeal, and, as the D.C. Circuit had for Paulette Barnes, it reinstated Tomkins's claim. The *Tomkins* appeals court defined the supervisor's sexual demands as "a condition of employment, an additional duty or burden Tomkins was required . . . to meet as a prerequisite to continued employment."[39] As for whether this additional burden was imposed because Tomkins was a woman, the court reiterated analyses developed by the district court in *Williams* and by the appeals court in *Barnes*: that the basis for discrimination need not be "peculiar to one of the genders" to be sex-based; and that while a person's sex must be a motivating factor, it need not be the only factor for a practice to violate Title VII.[40] Firmly stating the core elements of quid pro quo sexual harassment law, the *Tomkins* appeals court con-

35. *Barnes v. Costle*, at 990.
36. Ibid.
37. Ibid., at n. 55.
38. Ibid., at 991, 992.
39. *Tomkins v. Public Service Electric & Gas Co.*, at 1047 (1977).
40. Ibid., at 1047, 1048.

cluded: "Title VII is violated when a supervisor . . . makes sexual advances or demands toward a subordinate employee and conditions that employee's job status evaluation, continued employment, promotion, or other aspects of career development on a favorable response to those advances or demands."[41]

With the appellate decisions in *Barnes* and *Tomkins*, sexual extortion in employment moved squarely under the prohibitions of Title VII. As a judicially recognized problem of sex discrimination, sexual extortion would be reviewed by courts following rules that apply to all other disparate treatment cases — cases brought by women passed over for promotion by less qualified men, for example.[42] As with other disparate treatment cases, the core harm claimed by a plaintiff in a sexual harassment case would be that she (or he) was treated differently because she is a woman (or he is a man).

A sexual harassment target may state a quid pro quo claim if she can first show that an employment benefit has been conditioned — either implicitly or explicitly — on her compliance in an unwelcomed sexual activity. This is a prima facie case, and it must assemble facts that lead to an inference that discrimination has occurred. This phase of a case is first constructed from a woman's word. The employer then has an opportunity to prove either that no unwelcome sexual advance occurred or, if one did, that it carried no tangible consequences for the plaintiff's employment. Alternatively, the employer may argue that any adverse employment decision against the plaintiff had nothing to do with her response to the sexual advance and was not motivated by other discriminatory factors, such as her race or national origin. The plaintiff can counter by showing that the employer's denial of a sexual advance is untrue —"he said, she said"— and that the nondiscriminatory reason offered for the employment decision is a pretext for punishing her for refusing (or complaining about) the sexual advance. If the plaintiff prevails, Title VII requires her employer to provide equitable relief, such as

41. Ibid., at 1048–1049.

42. The framework for disparate treatment cases was developed in *McDonnell Douglas Corp. v. Green*, 411 U.S. 792, 804–5 (1973), and revised in *Texas Department of Community Affairs v. Burdine*, 450 U.S. 248, 253–54 (1981). *Henson v. City of Dundee*, 682 F. 2d. 897 (11th Cir., 1982), spelled out the framework in sexual harassment contexts.

back pay, reinstatement, or a lost promotion. With enactment of the Civil Rights Act of 1991, employers also became liable for compensatory and punitive damages up to $300,000, depending on the size of their workforce.[43]

The quid pro quo framework applied only to situations in which an implied or explicit sexual exchange was linked to a woman's employment status. Courts have interpreted the framework restrictively, usually requiring a plaintiff to demonstrate that tangibly adverse economic consequences resulted from her spurning of a supervisor's sexual advances. Paulette Barnes, Diane Williams, Adrienne Tomkins, and Margaret Miller all met this test: they were fired. What about Jane Corne and Geneva DeVane, though, who quit their jobs rather than endure sexual harassment? What about women who try to keep their jobs despite their bosses' sexual conduct? What about women who have no choice but to submit sexually because they need their wages? What about women whose damage is subjective and personal, not objectively economic? The quid pro quo theory does not reach across the spectrum of sexual harassment because it does not recognize that the primary injury of sexual harassment is that it forces women to accept sexual intimidation and exploitation as conditions of employment or education — or to resist those conditions at the cost of economic opportunity. The quid pro quo theory does not treat sexual harassment as discrimination *in itself*, finding discrimination only in its tangible consequences.

FINDING DISCRIMINATION
WHERE THE INJURY IS SUBJECTIVE

The challenge confronted by women seeking relief from sexual harassment has been to convince the courts not only that they have

43. Before 1991, no damages were available under Title VII. The 1991 Civil Rights Act provided capped damages: no more than $50,000 (combined compensatory and punitive) for employers with 15 to 100 employees; no more than $100,000 for employers with 101 to 200 employees; no more than $200,000 for employers with 201 to 500 employees; and no more than $300,000 for employers with more than 500 employees. 42 U.S.C. s1981a(b)(3).

been injured, but also that their injuries violate their civil rights. Congress did not discuss sexual harassment when it enacted Title VII in 1964, nor even in 1972 when it strengthened Title VII enforcement and affirmed its commitment to eliminating sex discrimination.[44] Not until 1990 did Congress devote sustained attention to the problem, and then only in the context of adding compensatory and punitive damages to Title VII remedies.[45] Congress has never legislated a definition of sexual harassment; neither has it attempted to specify its manifestations or the conditions for employer liability.[46] These silences match Congress's general silence about the precise forms discrimination may take. As the Fifth Circuit explained in its seminal ruling on racial harassment way back in 1971, "Congress chose neither to enumerate specific discriminatory practices, nor to elucidate in extenso the parameter of such nefarious activities. Rather, it pursued the path of wisdom by being unconstrictive, knowing that constant change is the order of our day and that the seemingly reasonable practices of the present can easily become the injustices of the morrow."[47]

In the absence of explicit Congressional direction, courts have charted the development of sexual harassment law according to what judges think about women's reactions to men's sexual conduct. When should women accept vulgarities as merely adolescent horseplay? When should we accept sexual solicitations as men's natural expressions of heterosexual desire? Such questions have challenged judges to distinguish among practices that primarily are just a part of life, though they may reflect or produce inequality, and practices that primarily enforce inequality, though they, too, are part of life.

44. Equal Employment Opportunity Act of 1972, P.L. 92-261, 86 Stat. 103 (1972); U.S. House of Representatives, Committee on Education and Labor, *Report No. 92-238*, 92nd Congress, 1st Session (Washington, D.C., 1971).

45. See, e.g., U.S. House of Representatives, *Civil Rights and Women's Equity in Employment Act of 1991*, House Report No. 102-40(I), Title II, Section 206 (April 24, 1991).

46. Even Senate Resolution 209 "Condemning Sexual Harassment" following the Anita Hill–Clarence Thomas hearings did not say what sexual harassment *is*. *Congressional Record*, S15291, S15298 (October 28, 1991).

47. *Rogers v. EEOC*, 454 F. 2d. 234, 238 (5th Cir., 1971), *cert. denied*, 1972.

The first big stumbling block to winning Title VII relief from sexual harassment was the common notion that men's expression of sexual desire was both natural and personal. This view conflated sexual desire with its expression, normalizing requests for prostitution (sex in exchange, for, say, better pay) as ordinary communication of attraction. Arguments developed by women's legal advocates in the early quid pro quo cases gradually illuminated the distinction between desire and its expression, leading some courts to comprehend that when the expression of desire mixes with official power in public institutions such as workplaces and schools, discrimination may occur. When presented with concrete punishments inflicted on women who rejected more powerful men's demands for sex, courts began to see that unwelcome sexual advances, pressures, or demands are discriminatory expressions of desire if a woman's employment or educational status is predicated on their satisfaction. Eventually, courts also understood that just as a woman would not be sexually harassed "but for her womanhood," a supervisor would not be in a position to extort sex "but for" the authority conferred on him by his employer. Thus did courts decide that employers are liable for sexual extortion of a subordinate by a supervisor.

The quid pro quo theory elaborated by courts established that punitive harassers discriminate against unwilling targets. The theory rests on judicial recognition of the power imbalance between superior and subordinate when the superior actually wields power against his target. The theory does not require an analysis of sexual harassment as a practice within a larger system of gender power, however. Instead, it focuses on individual sexual malfeasance, finding discrimination when that malfeasance produces detrimental objective consequences for one sex or the other.

The quid pro quo theory did not prepare courts to perceive the harm of sexual harassment when its costs could not be measured by tangible acts of differential treatment. Some supervisors may request sex, but without retaliating when they don't get it. Others may repeatedly ogle women, or comment on their breasts, or touch them deliberately in inappropriate places, but without ever demanding sex in exchange for a job benefit. Co-workers may direct demeaning sexual propositions to women or display pornography to ridicule and humiliate them, but without mixing workplace humiliation with employment power. Either supervisors or co-workers may hurl insults and innuendoes at one sex and not the other, but without producing injuries that can be verified objectively in absenteeism, doctor's bills, or disability claims. No less than does sexual extortion, these sorts of behaviors make sex women's burden at work or at school — telling each of us that we don't belong there, or at least not for the reasons we think we do. They comprise 90 percent of sexual harassment.[48]

In 1979, federal courts began to examine women's claims arising from the behaviors I've just described. Two bodies of precedent helped convince courts that sexual intimidation could be every bit as discriminatory as sexual extortion. First, the quid pro quo cases had already established that the sexual could be sex-based — that sexual conduct could single out members of one sex for differential treatment. Second, by 1979, the EEOC and the courts had had a decade of experience with race-based workplace intimidation complaints. Extortion — quid pro quo harassment — is unique to sex discrimination, as there is no real parallel for race or religion. Sexual intimidation, however, bears a family resemblance to the intimidation of workers (or students) on other discriminatory grounds. Hence courts

48. The U.S. Merit Systems Protection Board studied sexual harassment among federal workers in 1981 and 1987. The 1987 study found that 42 percent of female federal employees had experienced some form of unwanted and uninvited sexual attention. The 1981 study reported that 33 percent of women received unwanted sexual remarks; 28 percent received suggestive looks; 26 percent were inappropriately touched; 15 percent were pressured for dates; 9 percent were directly pressured for sexual favors; 9 percent received unwanted letters and phone calls; and 1 percent had been raped or sexually assaulted. In 1985, a landmark study based on random telephone interviews found that approximately half of the civilian women workers polled had experienced sexual harassment: degrading, insulting comments, 15 percent; sexual touching, 24 percent; socializing expected as part of the job requirement, 11 percent; expected sexual activity, 8 percent. http://www.inform.umd.edu/EdRes/Topic/WomensStudies/GenderIssues/SexualHarassment/NYTaskForceReport/chapter04, The Governor's Task Force on Sexual Harassment, *Sexual Harassment: Building a Consensus for Change*, Final Report Submitted to Governor Mario M. Cuomo (December 1993).

could borrow the logic of racial harassment law to scrutinize sexualized intimidation and humiliation.

From 1969 forward, EEOC decisions had obliged employers to maintain a workplace atmosphere free of racial intimidation or insult; decisions had held them liable for creating or maintaining an intolerable atmosphere.[49] In June 1970, for example, the EEOC determined that the owner of a beauty shop had violated Title VII because he had directed racial epithets at his African American manicurist; had stoked race hate by spreading rumors of a possible bomb set by a "typical Black"; and had ridiculed his African American employees by presenting them with watermelons on their birthdays in contrast to the cake and cookies he presented white workers on their birthdays.[50]

By 1972, a federal appeals court had backed up the EEOC's view that Title VII guaranteed an employment *environment* free of race discrimination, just as it guaranteed employment *decisions* free of such discrimination. In *Rogers v. EEOC*, Josephine Chavez charged that her employer, Texas State Optical, maintained an offensive work environment in which Latino patients were segregated from Anglos and in which she was permitted to attend only to Latinos.[51] Unequivocal in its view that environmental discrimination is a concern of Title VII, the court found "that the relationship between an employee and his [sic] working environment is of such significance as to be entitled to statutory protection."[52] Elaborating on this significance, the court explained: "Time was when employment discrimination tended to be viewed as a series of isolated and distinguishable events, manifesting itself, for example, in an employer's practices of hiring, firing, and promoting. But today employment discrimination is a far more complex and pervasive phenomenon, as the nuances and subtleties of discriminatory employment practices are no longer con-

49. Equal Employment Opportunity Commission, Decision No. YSF9-108 (June 26, 1969); Decision No. CL68-12-431EU (December 16, 1969); Decision No. 70-683 (April 10, 1970).

50. Equal Employment Opportunity Commission, Decision No. 71-2598 (June 22, 1970).

51. *Rogers v. EEOC*, at 237.

52. Ibid., at 238.

fined to bread and butter issues. . . . One can readily envision working environments so heavily polluted with discrimination as to destroy completely the emotional and psychological stability of minority group workers."[53]

This landmark decision effectively expanded Title VII's phrase "terms, conditions, or privileges of employment" to include the quality of the working environment. Under *Rogers*, Title VII did not promise workers an intimidation-free environment, any more than it promised workers that the workplace would be free of exploitation. What it did promise, according to *Rogers*, was that whatever burdens workers bore in the workplace must be born by workers regardless of race.

With *Griggs v. Duke Power Co.*,[54] which inspected the discriminatory effects of an employment practice rather than the discriminatory motivation of its practitioner, *Rogers* introduced a more sophisticated understanding of discrimination into Title VII law, one that permitted examination of systemic, institutionalized, and relational aspects of discrimination. When the *Rogers* court recognized that discrimination may involve more than "bread and butter issues," it introduced the notion that Title VII applies equally to the tangible *and* intangible manifestations of discrimination.

After *Rogers*, a number of courts sustained the view that Title VII does not require a showing of tangible economic loss to prove discrimination.[55] In 1973, for example, the court of appeals for the Eighth Circuit ruled that the "indignities of segregation" were sufficient to establish a Title VII violation, whether or not the jobs assigned to white workers in a segregated workplace were more economically desirable than those assigned to Blacks.[56] Other deci-

53. Ibid.

54. *Griggs v. Duke Power Company*, 401 U.S. 424 (1971). *Griggs* removes intent as the gravamen of disparate impact cases. Harassment cases do not fall under the *Griggs* framework, as they are disparate treatment cases that presume discriminatory intent.

55. E.g., *Swint v. Pullman Standard*, 539 F. 2d. 77, 90 (5th Cir., 1976). Examples drawn from Linda F. Thome, *Brief of the Women's Legal Defense Fund as Amicus Curiae, Bundy v. Jackson*, 641 F. 2d. 934 (D.C. Cir., 1979).

56. *Reed v. Arlington Hotel Corporation*, 476 F. 2d. 721, 726 (8th Cir., 1973).

sions established that employment practices totally unrelated to a worker's job status — such as segregated bathrooms — were racially discriminatory.[57]

Underpinning *Rogers's* finding that the workplace environment implicated equality of employment opportunity was its assertion that harassment can make or break a worker's environment. *Rogers* left open the question, however, of *when* intimidating racist conduct becomes racial discrimination. After *Rogers*, some courts did reject discrimination claims based on "a mere utterance of an ethnic or racial epithet which engenders offensive feelings in an employee."[58] But no court refuted the *Rogers* holding that racial harassment in itself can be a form of race-based discrimination in employment when it creates a hostile environment. Women plaintiffs and feminist legal advocates thus had a body of law to draw from in their efforts to expand the concept of sexual harassment to include situations in which the effects of unwanted sexual attention or abuse are not quantifiable or palpable, though they can be psychologically costly and make it more difficult for a woman to do her job.[59]

The first court to decide that sexual harassment creates a discriminatory environment — that sexual harassment is "illegal in itself"[60]— quoted extensively from *Rogers* to explain why the job environment is a "condition of employment" governed by Title VII.[61]

57. *James v. Stockham Valves & Fittings*, 559 F. 2d. 310, 319–20 (5th Cir., 1977), *cert. denied*, 1978.

58. *Rogers v. EEOC*, at 238, distinguishing environmental harassment from a single verbal insult. An often-cited decision that refused to find discriminatory harassment in an isolated incident was *Carridi v. Kansas City Chiefs Football Club*, 568 F. 2d. 87 (8th Cir., 1977).

59. By the time *Bundy* was argued, numerous cases had successfully alleged a racially hostile work environment: e.g., *Calcote v. Texas Educational Foundation, Inc.*, 458 F. Supp. 231 (W.D. Tex., 1976) (racial harassment of a white employee created discriminatory working conditions); *Firefighters Institute for Racial Equality v. City of St. Louis*, 549 F. 2d. 506 (segregated eating clubs created a discriminatory work environment for Blacks); *Lucero v. Beth Israel Hospital & Geriatric Center*, 479 F. Supp. 452 (D. Colo., 1979) (numerous racial slurs created a discriminatory work environment for Blacks).

60. *Bundy v. Jackson*, 641 F. 2d. 934, 948 (D.C. Cir., 1981).

61. Ibid., at 943–945.

Citing numerous decisions since *Rogers* that had condemned racism in the work environment, the D.C. Court of Appeals reasoned in *Bundy v. Jackson*, "How then can sexual harassment, which injects the most demeaning sexual stereotypes into the general work environment and which always represents an intentional assault on an individual's innermost privacy, not be illegal?"[62]

"Moreover," the court continued, "an important principle articulated in *Rogers* . . . suggests the special importance of allowing women to sue to prevent sexual harassment without having to prove that they resisted the harassment and that their resistance caused them to lose tangible job benefits."[63] According to the court, if sexual harassment is discriminatory only when women suffer economically from it, "an employer could sexually harass a female with impunity by carefully stopping short of firing the employee or taking any other tangible actions against her in response to her resistance."[64] The court further argued that since the precondition for a tangibly adverse employment action is that a woman resist sexual advances, no woman who cannot prove she resisted will ever be considered to have been sexually harassed. Expressing its concern for the subtleties of coercion in the employment hierarchy, the court concluded: "So long as the employer never literally forces sexual relations on the employee, 'resistance' may be a meaningless alternative for her. If the employer demands no response to his verbal or physical gestures other than good-natured tolerance . . . [he] can . . . implicitly and effectively make the employee's endurance of sexual intimidation a 'condition' of her employment . . . with little hope of legal relief."[65]

With the Women's Legal Defense Fund and the EEOC as *amici curiae*, Sandra Bundy had appealed to the D.C. Circuit for precisely this kind of ruling. Although her claim began with a quid pro quo charge, she asked the court on appeal also to decide that "an employer violates Title VII merely by subjecting female employees to sexual harassment."[66] The appeals court deferred to the trial court

62. Ibid., at 945.
63. Ibid.
64. Ibid.
65. Ibid., at 946.
66. Ibid., at 938.

on the facts of the quid pro quo claim, in which Bundy alleged that one job promotion had been delayed because she had rebuffed her supervisors' sexual propositions and that a second had been denied because she had complained about them. Her employer insisted that she had not been promoted as quickly as she had wanted because her qualifications and job performance had not warranted it. Finding that Bundy had been "only marginally qualified . . . [and] was selected under the Department's Affirmative Action efforts," the district court affirmed the employer's assertion that Bundy's work had been deficient.[67] Bundy contested the lower court ruling, but the appeals court remanded her claim rather than decide it. What the appeals court did decide was that whether or not it had adversely affected Bundy's promotion, the behavior to which she had been subjected had created a discriminatory work environment. This opened a new phase of sexual harassment's legal history.

Taking a narrow view of what constitutes a "term or condition of employment," the district court had focused its inquiry on the connection between Sandra Bundy's refusal of her supervisors' sexual requests and her employment status. It found none. The district court did not dispute Bundy's allegation that sexual requests had been made; in fact, it concluded that the "allegations with regard to improper sexual advances . . . is [sic] fully proved."[68] A vocational rehabilitation specialist with the District of Columbia Department of Corrections, Bundy had endured sexual propositions from four superiors over a period of three years beginning in 1972. In January 1975, she complained to her ultimate supervisor about the sexual favors her other supervisors had requested of her. On hearing her story, this supervisor told her, "I want to take you to bed myself" and "any man in his right mind would want to rape you."[69]

The district court viewed this last remark as evidence that the supervisor did not take Bundy's complaint seriously. The court considered it a sign of levity, not discrimination, attributing such levity to the fact that Bundy's "superiors appeared to consider the making of

67. Finding of Fact No. 13, *Bundy v. Jackson*, 1979 WL 197 (D.D.C., 1979).
68. *Bundy v. Jackson* (1979).
69. Ibid., Finding of Fact Nos. 36 and 37, at 4.

improper sexual advances to female employees as standard operating procedure, a fact of life, a normal condition of employment in the office." Far from being troubled by this, the court observed, "it also appears that plaintiff's superiors did not consider [her] rejection of their improper sexual advances as a reason for . . . taking adverse action against her. It was a game played by the male superiors . . . you won some and you lost some."[70] Presumably concluding that if sexual harassment is no big deal to its perpetrators it should be no big deal to its targets, the court further maintained that since Bundy had not complained sooner, she had not taken the harassment "as serious — annoying, perhaps, but not serious." To support its point, the court declared: "It can be inferred from the evidence that plaintiff made a formal complaint in the matter primarily as a means of obtaining advancement."[71]

The appeals court zeroed in on the district court's assertion that sexual harassment in Bundy's workplace was "standard operating procedure, a fact of life, a normal condition of employment" that did not discriminate against women. Overturning the lower court on this point, it established that sexual harassment is not a singular practice but a continuum of practices, all of which are discriminatory because they create an intimidating or humiliating environment, not because they necessarily lead to loss of a job, a cut in pay, or similar negative economic impact. The hostile environment concept thus emerged from the *Bundy* appeal not as a distinct theory of sexual harassment but as an explanation for why sexual harassment itself is discrimination, even if its perpetrators do not intend its various effects. *Bundy* shifted the inquiry in sexual harassment cases from "can sexual conduct itself be discriminatory?" to "*when* is sexual conduct discriminatory?" and from "can you prove an economic loss?" to "*how* did it alter the terms and conditions of your employment?"

Bundy was decided in 1981, soon after the EEOC promulgated its first *Guidelines on Sexual Harassment in the Workplace.*[72] Building on

70. Ibid., Finding of Fact No. 38, at 4.
71. Ibid., Finding of Fact No. 47, at 6.
72. Equal Employment Opportunity Commission, *Guidelines on Discrimination Based on Sex*, 45 Fed. Reg. 74676–74677 (1980), 29 CFR Part 1604, Section 1604.11. The final *Guidelines* were issued in November 1980.

Bundy and the *Guidelines*, the Eleventh Circuit elaborated the elements of a successful hostile environment claim the following year in an appeal brought by Barbara Henson, a police dispatcher. The district court judgment had denied Henson's claim against the police chief, who she alleged had subjected her to demeaning sexual inquiries, vulgarities, and sexual advances over a two-year period.[73] Overturning the lower court's ruling that there can be no discrimination without a tangible job detriment, the appeals court spelled out the conditions under which an environmental discrimination claim could prevail. Such a claim would have to show that: (1) the plaintiff belongs to a group covered by Title VII's prohibition on discrimination, in this case a sex-based group (i.e., the plaintiff is either a woman or a man); (2) she was subjected to "unwelcome sexual harassment" as defined by the EEOC's *Guidelines*, meaning "sexual advances, requests for sexual favors, and other verbal or physical conduct of a sexual nature"; (3) she was singled out for this treatment because of her sex, which the *Henson* court presumed to be easily established except in cases of bisexual harassment; (4) the harassment affected the terms and conditions of her employment, namely, created an abusive work environment; and (5) the employer is responsible for the hostile environment.[74] This formulation remains the basic guide to hostile environment adjudication today.

It mirrors the basic guide for quid pro quo analysis, in that complaint-worthy sexual conduct must be unwelcome and must arise because of a worker's membership in a sex classification. Beyond these two elements, however, the hostile environment scheme imposes different factual requirements on plaintiffs that can make Title VII relief difficult to reach. While both quid pro quo and hostile environment claimants are required to show that the unwelcome conduct adversely affected a term or condition of employment, the adverse impact in a quid pro quo case is easily demonstrated by evidence of a quantifiable economic loss. The questions in a quid pro quo case are whether an economic loss occurred — a question that can be answered empirically — and whether the plaintiff's response to unwelcome sexual conduct directly caused that loss. A hostile environment

73. *Henson v. City of Dundee*, 683 F. 2d. 897 (11th Cir., 1982).
74. Ibid., at 903–905.

case considers both job-related and psychological effects of unwelcome sexual conduct on the plaintiff. At issue in a hostile environment case is whether such effects were detrimental, not whether they were concrete or directly attributable to an employer's decision.

In a hostile environment situation, the loss suffered by a target of sexual harassment is the quality of the workplace atmosphere. The question for the court to decide, then, is whether working conditions have been altered sufficiently to justify a charge of discrimination. To avoid situations in which a "mere utterance . . . which engenders offensive feelings" triggers legal action, the *Henson* court offered an egregiousness threshold for environmental violations of Title VII. It established that conduct must be "sufficiently severe and persistent to affect seriously the psychological well-being of employees" for a hostile environment claim to prevail.[75] The court left it to individual courts to determine what kind of conduct is "severe" and when it becomes "persistent" based "on the totality of the circumstances" in specific cases.[76] It also left it to individual courts to decide when a harassment target's psychological well-being has been "seriously" affected.

The subjective application of *Henson's* subjective standard produced wildly different verdicts from different judges. Sometimes women won relief. For example, one district court held that the U.S. Steel Corporation maintained a hostile environment because a supervisor made sexual advances toward a woman subordinate, telling her she would be "good in bed," and repeatedly probed into her personal life, asking about her dating habits and her views on oral sex.[77] At other times, women were denied relief, such as when a court concluded that three sex-related incidents were "not sufficiently pervasive,"[78] or when another court held that five instances of verbal sexual harassment by a supervisor over a three-year period did not create a "pattern of harassment . . . repeated to the point where it is 'routine' or 'of a generalized nature.'"[79] Yet another court decided that physi-

75. Ibid., at 904.
76. Ibid.
77. *Ambrose v. U.S. Steel Corporation*, 39 FEP Cases 30, 34–35 (D. Calif., 1985).
78. *Jones v. Flagship International*, 793 F. 2d. 714 (5th Cir., 1986).
79. *Downes v. F.A.A.*, 775 F. 2d. 288 (Fed. Cir., 1985).

cal touching, indecent propositions, obscene and lewd comments, and use of profanity "were random, sometimes meaningless encounters,"[80] not the ingredients of a sexually hostile environment.

Under *Henson*, hostile environment cases presented an additional difficulty beyond deciding just how hostile a work environment really is. According to *Henson*, whether an employer is liable for the behavior that turns the work environment hostile is an open question. In the quid pro quo situation, the employer's liability is automatic, once a tangible job consequence that is causally connected to unwelcome sexual conduct is proved. This is because the quid pro quo situation is one of sexual extortion, in which employment power is both apparent and deployed. In contrast, a hostile environment plaintiff might well prove that she was the target of intimidating sexual conduct and that it altered her work environment, but without being able to hold her employer responsible for it. If she cannot hold her employer responsible, she cannot claim Title VII remedies.

The EEOC's 1980 *Guidelines* held employers "responsible for its acts and those of its agents and supervisory employees with respect to sexual harassment."[81] According to *Henson*, however, employers were responsible only if they "knew or should have known" about the harassment and "failed to take prompt remedial action."[82] *Henson* applied this standard even to harassment by supervisors, if the harassment was not linked to an adverse employment decision. In the view of the *Henson* court, a plaintiff could prove that her employer "knew or should have known" about her harassment with evidence that she had complained about it. Alternatively, if she could show that the unwelcome sexual conduct was pervasive, that would suggest that the employer was aware of it, or ought to have been.[83]

The *Henson* decision, while ratifying the hostile environment concept, introduced high hurdles between sexual harassment targets and Title VII relief. The "severe and persistent" criterion imposed a subjective standard on a subjective injury, without providing guidance on how to apply the standard or from whose point of view. The

80. *Wimberly v. Shoney's Inc.*, 39 FEP Cases 444, 453 (S.D. Ga., 1985).
81. EEOC *Guidelines*, Section 1604.11(c).
82. *Henson v. City of Dundee*, at 905.
83. Ibid.

"knew or should have known" criterion for employer liability eliminated the distinction drawn by the EEOC between environmental harassment by supervisors, on the one hand, and by co-workers, on the other.

The EEOC had taken the view that liability follows power. In this view, harassment by co-workers becomes discrimination only when the employer creates, condones, or permits it to continue — when the employer is put on notice, or when it "knew or should have known." In contrast, because harassment by supervisors applies coercion derived from the employment hierarchy even if no employment action is taken by the supervisor, when a supervisor discriminates against a woman by sexually harassing her, it is as if the employer itself discriminated. The EEOC accordingly had considered employers liable for all discriminatory acts of their supervisors, whether tangible or intangible and whether or not the employer knew about them. *Henson* established that a sexual harassment target whose injuries were subjective would have to prove that her employer was liable before her harassment would count as discrimination, even if her harasser was her supervisor.

The first sexual harassment case to reach the Supreme Court presented an employer's appeal of a hostile environment claim that had been decided by principles far less restrictive than those devised by the *Henson* court. Indicating conflict among the circuits on sexual harassment issues, three years after *Henson* the Court of Appeals for the D.C. Circuit (the same court that had decided *Bundy*) ruled in *Vinson v. Taylor* that employers are always automatically liable for sexual harassment by their supervisory personnel.[84] Meritor Savings Bank, the employer, challenged this conclusion, arguing that harassment that is sexual (as opposed to racial) is "special" and "personal," at least when it does not affect employment decisions.[85] Thus, the bank maintained, it was not responsible for environmental harassment, even by supervisors. Besides, the bank continued, in this particular case, the sexual relations now called harassment had once been "voluntary."

84. *Vinson v. Taylor*, 753 F.2d. 141 (D.C. Cir., 1985).
85. Patricia J. Barry and Catharine A. MacKinnon, *Brief, Meritor Savings Bank v. Vinson*, 477 U.S. 57 (1986), 15–16.

Mechelle Vinson, a bank teller, brought this case against Sidney Taylor, a bank manager, alleging that over four years he had subjected her repeatedly to sexual pressure and rape. Out of fear of losing her job, she had acquiesced to sex forty or fifty times, until he stopped asking when she found a steady boyfriend. During the four years of harassment, she had been promoted several times, and although she ultimately was fired, it ostensibly was for taking too much leave, not for refusing Taylor's advances.

The Supreme Court rejected the bank's argument that Title VII did not apply to Mechelle Vinson's situation because it only covered discrimination of "an economic character."[86] Pointing to the EEOC's sexual harassment guidelines and to *Rogers* and its progeny, the Court affirmed the *Bundy* and *Henson* courts' conclusion that sexual harassment spans a continuum from extortion to intimidation to humiliation and that only sometimes does it involve economic effects. With *Meritor*, the question of *whether* a sexually hostile work environment defies Title VII was put to rest. After *Meritor*, however, courts would still have to decide *when* sexual conduct creates a hostile environment. This question in turn pivots on three others: whether the conduct is unwelcome, whether it is severe or pervasive, and what kind of liability principles apply to particular situations.

The Court's opinion in *Meritor* was rather abbreviated, considering this was its first sexual harassment case. The Court's brevity made for lapses in explanation and definition, which delegated interpretive authority to the lower courts that would hear most cases. One result has been conflict among the circuits (how does a woman prove she was offended? when is a single incident severe enough to count as harassment?) and an inconsistency in women's access to Title VII relief from sexual harassment. Another result has been suspicion on the streets and in corporate corridors that sexual harassment law is so murky that anyone can bring a charge and that a charge made is practically a charge proven. While uncertainty and fear can give incentive to employers to prevent sexual harassment through education and to deal efficiently with complaints through effective grievance procedures — to avoid lawsuits — the downside of uncertainty

86. *Meritor Savings Bank v. Vinson*, at 64.

and fear is the view that all workplace interactions between the sexes must be neutered.[87]

WHEN DOES SEXUAL CONDUCT BECOME HARASSMENT, AND WHEN DOES HARASSMENT BECOME DISCRIMINATION?

Quoting *Henson*, the Supreme Court in *Meritor* established unequivocally that "[s]exual harassment which creates a hostile or offensive environment for members of one sex is every bit the arbitrary barrier to sexual equality at the workplace that racial harassment is to racial equality." While the analogy to racial harassment had opened the way to Title VII review of sexual harassment, however, the analogy stretched a bit thin when it came to deciding when women have been sexually harassed. Even sexual insults and intimidation that resemble racial ones — such as calling a woman "slut" or "cunt" — have not been smoothly enfolded into the discrimination framework drawn by racial harassment law. As the EEOC cautioned in its *amicus* brief in *Meritor*, "Whereas racial slurs are intrinsically offensive and presumptively unwelcome, sexual advances and innuendo are ambiguous: depending on their context, they may be intended by the initiator, and perceived by the recipient, as denigrating or complimentary, as threatening or welcome, as malevolent or innocuous."[88] Examining a woman's behavior to resolve these ambiguities, some courts have found that a target's participation in sexual or profane banter proves that she either welcomed her harassment or could not have been offended by it.[89]

87. In 1996, 89 percent of U.S. companies had some sort of sexual harassment policy, up from 75 percent in 1991. A 1998 poll of U.S. workers reported that more than 84 percent had been informed by their companies of what to do if sexual harassment or discrimination problems arise. Amy Goldstein and Barbara Vobejda, "Companies, Courts Differ in Defining Harassment; Jones Case Highlights Stricter Standards," *Washington Post*, April 5, 1998; http://www.prnewswire.com, PR Newswire, "Employee Awareness of Sexual Harassment Policies and How to Report Violations Is High, Survey Shows," December 3, 1998.

88. Equal Employment Opportunity Commission, *Brief Amici Curiae, Meritor Savings Bank v. Vinson*, at 13.

89. E.g., *Reed v. Shepard*, 939 F. 2d. 484, 486–7 (7th Cir., 1991), finding that plaintiff JoAnn Reed "not only experienced . . . depravity with amazing

Like sexual slurs, unwanted sexual advances, requests for sexual favors, or demeaning sexual inquiries and suggestions all intrude on a woman's intimate personhood. Early courts had fastened on the personal aspects of such sexual conduct to deny that sexual conduct can be discrimination. Their focus had been the personal expressions of desire by individual men. When appeals courts and eventually the Supreme Court found discrimination in certain sexual conduct, they continued to emphasize the personal nature of harassment. But they shifted their attention from the personal actions of individual men to the personal reactions and wishes of individual women. This was an important change, for it eliminated a man's intent as an excuse for his behavior.[90]

At the same time, however, the focus on women's personal reactions rewarded defendants' inquiry into the personal qualities of the woman making a sexual harassment claim.[91] While federal rules of evidence have impeded excruciating scrutiny of plaintiffs' character or prior sexual history, courts often have permitted examination of the personal behaviors of plaintiffs where, when, or with whom they say their harassment occurred. For example, some circuits have allowed defendants to introduce evidence that a plaintiff is foul-mouthed or has traded dirty jokes with male co-workers to establish that she could not have been offended by the alleged harassment.[92]

---

resilience, but she also relished reciprocating in kind. At one point during her job tenure Reed was actually put on probation for her use of offensive language at the jail. . . . [T]he conclusion . . . must be that plaintiff participated freely in many of these antics and in fact instigated some of them." See also, *Vermett v. Hough*, 627 F. Supp. 587 (W.D. Mich., 1986).

90. "Federal laws prohibiting racial and sexual harassment are wholly uninterested in the perpetrator's intent." *Jones v. Commander, Kansas Army Ammunitions Plant*, 147 F.R.D. 248 (D.C. Kansas, 1993).

91. Susan Estrich, "Sex at Work," *Stanford Law Review* 43 (1991): 827–828; Jacqueline H. Sloan, "Extending Rape Shield Protection to Sexual Harassment Actions: New Federal Rule of Evidence 412 Undermines *Meritor Savings Bank v. Vinson*," *Southwestern University Law Review* 25 (1996): 363–401.

92. *Swentek v. USAir, Inc.*, 830 F. 2d. 552 (4th Cir., 1987); *Katz v. Dole*, 709 F. 2d. 251 (4th Cir., 1983), discussed in Sloan, "Extending Rape Shield Protection to Sexual Harassment." See also, *Reed v. Shepard*, n. 89 supra.

Some state courts have admitted evidence of a plaintiff's prior affectionate social contact with a defendant to undermine her claim that he harassed her.[93] One federal district court ruled that if a defendant knows about a plaintiff's past sexual conduct with other employees, he may introduce that information at trial.[94] This sort of attention to women's conduct and character means that the strength of a harassment claim often depends on who is bringing it.

One way to avoid this casuistry would be to say that if a woman complains about it, the sexual conduct was by definition offensive, and if she was offended by it, then she was harassed. A complainant may have to cross other thresholds to gain legal remedies for her harassment (was it severe or pervasive? did the employer know?) but the complaint itself would dispel questions about whether she suffered harassment in the first place. The Supreme Court did not adopt this approach in *Meritor*. Instead, it held that "[t]he gravamen of any sexual harassment claim is that the alleged sexual advances were 'unwelcome' . . . [and] [t]he trier of fact must determine the existence of sexual harassment in light of 'the record as a whole' and 'the totality of circumstances, such as the nature of the sexual advances and the context in which the alleged incidents occurred.'"[95]

The *Meritor* court expressly stated that information about a plaintiff's "provocative dress" or "sexual fantasies" are "obviously relevant" to ascertaining the context in which sexual advances were made.[96] In turn, the Court implied that the context — the "totality of circumstances" — could offset a claim that sexual advances had been unwelcome: sort of a "she asked for it" defense. Importantly, the Court nowhere asserted that a plaintiff's prior sexual history could decide the welcomeness of the sexual conduct at issue.[97] In hostile environment cases, as in quid pro quo cases, it did insist, however,

93. *Kresko v. Rulli*, 432 N.W. 2d. 764 (Minn. Ct. App., 1988), discussed in Sloan.

94. *Weiss v. Amoco Oil Co.*, 142 F.R.D. 311 (S.D. Iowa, 1992), discussed in Sloan.

95. *Meritor Savings Bank v. Vinson*, at 68–69.

96. Ibid., at 69.

97. Neither did the Court forbid inquiry into a plaintiff's sexual history, however, leaving the issue to be sorted through by judges with guidance from federal rules of evidence.

that a plaintiff show that she *never* wanted the attention she is complaining about, not that she just doesn't want it now. Further, by suggesting a nexus between a woman's conduct and sexual advances, insults, or humiliation, the Court created a loophole for defendants. Under *Meritor*, alleged harassers have sought and offered evidence to show that because their targets have uttered vulgarities or have been receptive to other men's sexual overtures, they could not have been offended by *theirs*. Not all courts have entertained this evidence.[98] But most courts have interpreted *Meritor* to require that they at least consider a woman's "sexually provocative" dress, speech, or fantasies when assessing the welcomeness and offensiveness of an alleged harasser's conduct, even if many have limited the weight of such evidence.[99]

The Court's declaration that a woman's behavior is "obviously relevant" put the decision about whether a woman has been harassed in the hands of the court, not in the hands of the woman. There was a silver lining to this element of the Court's decision, however. The reason the Court reached the unwelcomeness issue was that it sought to remove a woman's apparently voluntary compliance with sexual demands as a bar to stating a sexual harassment claim. According to the district court in *Meritor*, any sexual relationship between Mechelle Vinson and Sidney Taylor had been a "voluntary" one that had nothing to do with Vinson's employment.[100] According to Mechelle Vinson, however, she had acquiesced to sex out of fear of a job-related reprisal. Echoing the *Bundy* appeals court's argument against a resistance requirement for sexual harassment plaintiffs, the Supreme Court found it plausible that some subordinates may feel coerced into granting sexual favors because of a superior's employment power. Hence, "[t]he correct inquiry is whether [Vinson], by her conduct, indicated that the alleged sexual advances were unwelcome, not whether her actual participation in sexual intercourse was voluntary."[101]

98. E.g., *Priest v. Rotary*, 98 F.R.D. 755, 762 (N.D. Cal., 1983); *Burns v. McGregor Electronics Industries, Inc.*, 989 F. 2d. 959, 963 (8th Cir., 1993).

99. E.g., *Mitchell v. Hutchings*, 116 F.R.D. 481, 486 (D. Utah, 1987); *Swentek v. USAir, Inc.* (1987), at 557.

100. *Meritor Savings Bank v. Vinson*, at 61.

101. Ibid., at 68.

Yet, even demonstrably unwelcome sexual conduct is not necessarily prohibited by Title VII. If an employer is not liable for the conduct, it escapes Title VII review. The *Meritor* court rejected the appeals court's holding that an employer is automatically liable for a hostile environment created by a supervisor's sexual advances.[102] But it did not resolve the liability issue by substituting an alternative framework. What the Court did say was that although an employer is not automatically liable just because harassment occurs in its workplace, neither is it automatically exempt from liability just because it has a grievance procedure and a policy against harassment.[103] Further, the Court said that the fact that an employer has not been informed of the harassment does not automatically shield it from liability. But the Court did not decide when employers are liable in hostile environment cases, stating only that "Congress wanted courts to look to agency principles for guidance in this area."[104] Until 1998, courts generally held employers liable for hostile environments created by sexual harassment if they knew or should have known about the harassment and failed to take prompt action to end and remedy it. This standard has been applied in hostile environment cases even when supervisors harass subordinates. Many women have been deprived of redress under Title VII as a result, because their position on the employment hierarchy discourages telling about the harassment and because this is the classic "he said, she said" situation that employers rarely witness.

The *Meritor* court also deferred a definitive ruling on when unwelcome sexual conduct that an employer "knew or should have known about" actually creates a discriminatory environment. Reasoning that "not all workplace conduct that may be described as 'harassment' affects a 'term, condition, or privilege' of employment," the Court agreed with *Henson* that "[f]or sexual harassment to be actionable, it must be sufficiently severe or pervasive 'to alter the conditions of [the victim's] employment and create an abusive working environment.'"[105] It is crucial to note that while it concurred in general

102. Ibid., at 69–70.
103. Ibid., at 72.
104. Ibid.
105. Ibid., at 67.

with *Henson*, the *Meritor* court also changed the *Henson* standard for actionable conduct. *Henson* required that the conduct be "severe *and* persistent."[106] *Meritor* required that it be "severe *or* pervasive."[107] This opened the possibility that a few — or even one — severe incidents of unwelcome sexual conduct could satisfy the threshold for a discrimination claim, depending on the "totality of the circumstances."

Under the *Meritor* decision, some courts have found that a single incident of sufficient gravity can create a hostile environment.[108] This is especially true where physical conduct — touching, squeezing, pinching, grabbing, kissing, exposing oneself (not to mention raping) — is involved. The EEOC's *Policy Guidance on Sexual Harassment* supports this approach: "More so than in the case of verbal advances or remarks, a single unwelcome physical advance can seriously poison the victim's working environment. If an employee's supervisor sexually touches that employee, the [EEOC] normally would find a violation."[109] Also, some courts have ruled that the more hostile the conduct — the more misogynist or threatening the insults — the less frequent it needs to have been to create a discriminatory environment.[110] That said, there is no settled standard for reviewing single-incident sexual harassment, so ultimately it is up to individual judges and juries to decide whether the particular conduct in a given case is sufficiently severe to count as discrimination if it happened only once, or whether it needs to be pervasive.

Such discretion can yield results that not only are bizarre, but also are unfavorable to women. In 1990, for example, the Tenth Circuit held that a manager's suggestion to a subordinate that she "sit on his face" was "opprobrious and vulgar" but not something that "pervades and poisons the work atmosphere."[111] Some courts have even spared severe *and* pervasive conduct from liability under Title VII.

106. My italics.

107. My italics.

108. E.g., *Jones v. Wesco Investments*, 846 F. 2d. 1154 (8th Cir., 1988); *Watts v. New York City Police Department*, 724 F. Supp. 99 (S.D.N.Y., 1989).

109. Quoted in Barbara Lindemann and David D. Kadue, *Sexual Harassment in Employment Law* (Washington, D.C., 1992), 177.

110. Ibid., 178.

111. *Wolf v. Burum*, 1990 WL 81219 (D. Kan., 1990).

In 1995, for instance, the Seventh Circuit denied relief to a woman whose boss had harassed her during a period of seven months, regularly calling her a "pretty girl," making "um-um-um" grunting sounds when she wore a leather skirt to work, suggesting she run around naked, saying he couldn't control himself, and indicating masturbation with a gesture. According to Judge Richard Posner, "these incidents . . . could [not] reasonably be thought to add up to sexual harassment. . . . Mr. Hall . . . is not a man of refinement; but neither is he a sexual harasser. . . . He never said anything to her that could not be repeated on primetime television. . . . The reference to masturbation completes the impression of a man whose sense of humor took final shape in adolescence. It is no doubt distasteful to a sensitive woman to have such a silly man as one's boss, but only a woman of Victorian delicacy — a woman mysteriously aloof from contemporary American popular culture in all its sex-saturated vulgarity — would find Hall's patter substantially . . . distressing."[112]

How judges decide what does and doesn't count as discrimination depends on the criteria they employ to analyze disputes. Until 1993, some courts required plaintiffs to prove that they had been debilitated by the harassment — that the injury was not discrimination itself but its objective psychological consequences.

Courts also applied a "reasonableness" standard imported from tort law to decide whether discrimination had occurred. Under this standard, courts often assessed "unwelcomeness" and "offensiveness" from the perspective of the alleged harasser. Increasingly, courts examined the impact of a harasser's behavior on his target, as well, here requiring a plaintiff to show that the behavior would have affected others in the same way it affected her. Since 1991, the Ninth Circuit has examined cases from the "reasonable woman's" perspective, weighing a plaintiff's claim against how other women might have reacted in the same situation.[113] Other circuits have relied on the perspective of a hypothetical person who is both reasonable and genderless. Courts thus reject the idea that the only point of view that counts is that of the harassment target. Not only is the alleged ha-

112. *Baskerville v. Culligan International Co.*, 50 F. 3d. 428 (7th Cir., 1995).
113. *Ellison v. Brady*, 924 F. 2d. 8872 (9th Cir., 1991).

rasser's conduct on trial in a sexual harassment case, but also his target's mental state, as the injuries of discrimination are judged against the reasonableness of complaining about it.

The standard or criteria adopted by a court to evaluate a target's experience can cheat her of Title VII vindication. For example, in *Rabidue v. Osceola Refining Company*, decided shortly after *Meritor*, the Sixth Circuit determined that, to establish discrimination, a sexual harassment plaintiff must prove that the challenged conduct created a hostile environment "that affected seriously her psychological well-being" *and* that it disturbed her work performance.[114] A woman who continued to do a good job despite the harassment had no claim under this standard.

The *Rabidue* court adopted "the perspective of a reasonable person" to judge the effects of the sexual conduct Vivienne Rabidue had complained about. Focusing the "reasonableness" test on Vivienne Rabidue, the court asked whether her reactions were reasonable, that is, whether a "reasonable person" would have found her harasser's behaviors offensive and damaging to her work environment. It concluded that a workplace smeared with pornography in which a manager "routinely referred to women as 'whores,' 'cunt,' 'pussy,' and 'tits'" and specifically referred to the plaintiff as a "fat ass" and "bitch [who] needs . . . a good lay" was not a discriminatory environment, because "the evidence did not demonstrate that this single employee's vulgarity substantially affected the totality of the workplace."[115] In addition, the court asserted that the "psyches of the plaintiff or other female employees" could not have been seriously harmed "in the context of a society that condones and publicly features and commercially exploits open displays of . . . erotica." Furthermore, the court continued: "it cannot seriously be disputed that in some work environments, humor and language are rough hewn and vulgar. . . . Title VII was not meant to . . . change this. It must never be forgot-

114. Women's Legal Defense Fund and the National Women's Law Center, et al., *Brief as Amici Curiae in Support of Petitioner, Harris v. Forklift Systems*, 1992 U.S. Briefs 1168 (April 30, 1993) (LEXIS-NEXIS).

115. *Rabidue v. Osceola Refining Company*, 805 F. 2d. 611, 624 (6th Cir., 1986).

ten that Title VII is the federal court mainstay in the struggle for equal employment opportunity. . . . But it is quite different to claim that Title VII was designed to bring about a magical transformation in the social mores of American workers."[116]

Although *Meritor* had its limitations, it had been a real breakthrough for women who suffered harassment but who did not receive tangible demerits for their responses to it. *Rabidue* was a setback, at least in the Sixth Circuit. For one thing, the decision compounded the requirements to prove discrimination in hostile environment cases: there now needed to be tangible psychological evidence, sort of as an analogue to the tangible economic evidence marshaled in quid pro quo cases. For another, *Rabidue* maintained that a "hypothetical reasonable individual" would be so inured to misogyny just by living in society that she couldn't possibly be offended or debilitated by it in the workplace.

Seven years later, the Supreme Court would take the opportunity to correct *Rabidue*, or at least that part of it that required proof of tangible psychological harm. In *Harris v. Forklift Systems, Inc.*, the Court reviewed Teresa Harris's charge that the company president frequently directed gender-based insults at her, along with sexual innuendoes. On several occasions, the CEO told Harris, "You're a woman, what do you know" and "We need a man [for the job]."[117] Once, he told her she was "a dumb ass woman." Another time, he suggested she go with him "to the Holiday Inn to negotiate [her] raise." Occasionally, he asked Harris and other women subordinates to get coins from his front pants pocket or to pick up objects he had thrown on the ground in front of them.[118] When Harris complained to the CEO, he claimed he was "only joking" and promised to stop. But he resumed less than a month later, at which point Harris quit her job.[119]

The district court thought that the behavior Harris found offensive was not serious enough to affect her psychological well-being.

116. Ibid., at 620–621.
117. *Harris v. Forklift Systems, Inc.*, 510 U.S. 17, 19 (1993).
118. Ibid.
119. Ibid.

It explained that a "reasonable woman" also might have been offended, but her work performance would not have been impaired.[120] The *Rabidue* circuit upheld this verdict. The Supreme Court chose a "middle path" between making a federal case of *any* sexual conduct a woman deems offensive and depriving women of their right to state a case if they cannot show a tangible psychological injury. Repeating the "severe or pervasive" standard, the Court affirmed that conduct that does not create an objectively hostile or abusive work environment is beyond Title VII's grasp. However, the Court also insisted that "Title VII comes into play before the harassing conduct leads to a nervous breakdown. . . . [T]he very fact that the discriminatory conduct was so severe or pervasive that it created a work environment abusive to employees because of their race, gender, religion, or national origin offends Title VII's broad rule of workplace equality."[121]

The Court repeatedly referred to the effects of harassment on "reasonable persons" in explaining why sexual harassment is discriminatory regardless of whether its consequences are tangible. Women's legal advocates generally considered this a loss, either because they had wanted the Court to take the point of view of the "reasonable woman" or because they thought that adopting the perspective of ungendered outsiders would skew a fair review of what actually happened to a sexually harassed woman and how it affected her.[122] While the Court certainly did not hand women's advocates a victory on this score, neither did it definitively settle the issue. The Court's affirmation of a "reasonable person" standard does insult a woman's knowledge of her own harm. Still, the Court's adoption of the standard was more tacit than explicit and did not involve a refutation of arguments for either a "reasonable woman" standard or for no standard at all. More important, the Court also said that a woman's subjective view of her work environment matters, because it is she who decides in the first instance whether unwelcome sexual conduct has turned her workplace into a hostile, intimidating, or offensive place to be.

120. Ibid., at 20.
121. Ibid., at 22.
122. For an argument against a "reasonableness" standard, see Women's Legal Defense Fund, et al., *Brief as Amici Curiae*, 15–19.

The Court's rejection of the tangible psychological injury requirement asserted in *Rabidue* gave an unambiguous boost to sexual harassment plaintiffs. It lowered the egregiousness threshold imported from the quid pro quo context and adapted to hostile environment claims by *Henson*. Retreating from dramatic language inspired by the "appalling conduct" at issue in cases like *Meritor*, the *Harris* Court explained that "the reference . . . to environments 'so heavily polluted with discrimination as to destroy completely the emotional and psychological stability of minority group workers' . . . *merely present some especially egregious examples of harassment. They do not mark the boundary of what is actionable.*" [123]

This means that unwelcome sexual conduct does not have to be off the charts before women can seek Title VII relief from it. *Harris* thus made Title VII more accessible to targets of sexual harassment. It did this at the very time sexual harassment was becoming more expensive for employers.

Congress added a compensatory and punitive damages component to Title VII remedies in November 1991: women who prove they have been sexually harassed now can win monetary awards from juries. This change upped the ante for employers: the possibility of winning damages makes it hard for employers to induce plaintiffs to settle for token amounts, but fighting a claim all the way to a verdict can be even more costly.

Soon after the Congress created the monetary damages remedy for workplace discrimination, the Supreme Court extended the right to claim damages to plaintiffs in sexual harassment (and other sex discrimination) cases involving educational institutions. [124] These cases, often brought by students, arise under Title IX of the Education Act Amendments of 1972. When monetary damage awards became available under Title IX, sexual harassment claims became potentially very expensive for schools, colleges, and universities.

The increased stakes of sexual harassment liability intensified attention to sexual harassment in schools and workplaces. Most schools and companies now have sexual harassment policies and grievance

123. *Harris v. Forklift Systems, Inc.*, at 22.
124. *Franklin v. Gwinnett County Public Schools*, 503 U.S. 69 (1992).

procedures on the books, indicating at least token concern for the problem. As one sexual harassment counselor put it, however, "Pieces of paper that say things do not change the culture."[125]

Sexual harassment law permits targets to answer their harassers in a way that commands attention not only from individual perpetrators but also from officials and institutions that tolerate them. Ideally, each woman who answers her harasser helps to undermine the culture of sexualized inequality, for if it cannot change belief, sexual harassment law at least disciplines behavior. The culture of sexualized inequality is quite resilient, however. It resists the disciplinary incursions of sexual harassment law by exaggerating its risks. And it subjects women who use the law to a regime of disbelief.

The regime of disbelief is in the first instance a political one, but its effects reverberate through the law. Under the regime of disbelief, when women such as Anita Hill and Paula Jones reveal their harassment, some of the public wonders why they're talking about it, some of the public wonders whether it was bad enough to count, and some of the public wonders whether calling it harassment doesn't exaggerate trivial events or misconstrue innocuous ones. Given all this second-guessing, it is no wonder that an estimated 95 percent of sexual harassment incidents are never reported.[126] Until the political environment supports women's use of sexual harassment law, men's everyday use of sex to enforce women's inequality will continue.

125. Amy Goldstein and Barbara Vobejda, "Companies, Courts Differ in Defining Harassment: Jones Case Highlights Stricter Standards," *Washington Post*, April 5, 1998.

126. Barry S. Roberts and Richard A. Mann, "Sexual Harassment in the Workplace: A Primer," *Akron Law Review*, 29 (Winter 1996): 269, 271.

t h r e e **Toward a Better Day
in Court for Women?**

Most people have a sense of what sexual harassment is, and most agree that when sexual harassment occurs something should be done about it. Unfortunately, however, a too common reaction to a report of sexual harassment is to doubt that it occurred at all. Another common reaction is to hold women to very high thresholds for abuse, as if anything short of felonious assault is just a matter of miscommunication. President Clinton conveyed both reactions to the grand jury investigating his alleged perjury and obstruction of justice in the Paula Jones case. Explaining that sex is "the most mysterious area of human life," Clinton twice volunteered to the grand jury that he believed Anita Hill and Clarence Thomas both "thought they were telling the truth."[1] Following this logic, we can never decide whether sexual harassment really happened.

This sort of opportunistic relativism may sound distinctively Clintonian, but it is actually symptomatic of women's subordination under the regime of disbelief. Compelled to "believe Anita Hill" because he was supported by feminists, Clinton nonetheless could not believe her enough to disbelieve Clarence Thomas. To make such a choice would give too much weight to one woman's word. This would corrode the structural advantage enjoyed by harassers — power. If we really took women's words seriously, imagine how many men would be subject to scrutiny.

The structural advantage of harassers when they harass becomes a political advantage when they must defend or deny their actions. Harassers' political advantage discourages women — especially the most economically vulnerable women — from seeking the remedies the law says they are entitled to. Not surprisingly, despite ten years of dramatic advances in the law, when Anita Hill disclosed her experiences with Clarence Thomas in the fall of 1991, sexual harassment rates remained steady and high and few women had spoken publicly of their harassment.

As the Senate Judiciary Committee began its inquiry into Hill's allegations, the *New York Times* reported that 40 percent of women workers had received unwanted sexual advances or remarks from male supervisors.[2] Ten years earlier, a study of women who worked for the federal government had found that 43 percent had been subjected to harassment.[3] Such studies indicated that millions of women workers had been sexually harassed by 1990. Some surveys showed that millions of women — 15 percent of all women workers — were harassed *each year*.[4]

1. http://www.washtimes.com:80/investiga/investiga8.html, "Clinton's Grand Jury Testimony — Part Five," and "Clinton's Grand Jury Testimony — Part Six," *Washington Times*, September 21, 1998.

2. Elizabeth Kolbert, "Sexual Harassment at Work Is Pervasive, Survey Suggests," *New York Times*, October 11, 1991.

3. U.S. Merit Systems Protection Board, *Sexual Harassment of Federal Workers: Is It a Problem?* (Washington, D.C., 1981).

4. "Statement of Dr. Freada Klein Before the House Committee on Education and Labor," February 27, 1991 (author's files).

High rates of sexual harassment did not translate into large numbers of sexual harassment cases. The Equal Employment Opportunity Commission recorded an average of only 5,462 sexual harassment complaints in each of the four years following the 1986 *Meritor* decision.[5] It filed lawsuits in only fifty sexual harassment cases in 1990, in only fifty the year before, and in only forty-one the year before that.[6] The agency did issue "right to sue" letters permitting complainants to litigate on their own behalf; however, no more than one hundred cases a year actually made it to trial.[7] Clearly, although women had won legal weapons to fight harassment by 1991, those weapons were poorly — and scarcely — deployed.

Various barriers stood between women and their law. By the time Anita Hill disclosed her experiences with Clarence Thomas, the Reagan-Bush EEOC had controlled the implementation of sexual harassment law for nearly a dozen years. In fact, Thomas had chaired the EEOC for eight of those years — a tenure distinguished by his efforts to weaken Title VII enforcement policies generally and to shift the burden of proof in investigations to favor employers.[8] By 1986, the midpoint in Thomas's tenure, the EEOC was securing settlements in only 13.6 percent of the cases it closed (down from 32.1 percent in FY1980) and finding "no reasonable cause" to believe that discrimination had occurred in 56.6 percent of the cases it reviewed.[9] The agency's ideological climate and its reputation for inaction undoubtedly discouraged some women from reporting harassment.[10]

The relatively short statute of limitations for filing a claim under Title VII (within 180 days of the alleged act of discrimination) also

5. The EEOC reported 5,350 complaints in 1987; 5,231 in 1988; 5,572 in 1989; and 5,694 in 1990.

6. Tamar Lewin, "A Case Study of Sexual Harassment," *New York Times*, October 11, 1991.

7. Ibid.

8. Patricia Ireland, "Clarence Thomas Is a Threat to American Democracy and the Bill of Rights," *National Law Journal*, July 29, 1991, 17–18.

9. Jane Mayer and Jill Abramson, *Strange Justice: The Selling of Clarence Thomas* (Boston, 1994), 73, 143.

10. Referring to the EEOC's handling of age discrimination claims, one judge wrote that the agency "has at best been slothful, at worst deceptive to the public." Quoted in ibid.

impeded complaints because many women's first inclination is to struggle privately with as intimate a form of discrimination as sexual harassment.[11] Especially in hostile environment cases, where the direct consequences of harassment are not tangibly economic, a woman initially might try to cope with her harassment rather than complain about it — and thus could allow the clock to run out. Many women who did meet the statutory timetable became disheartened by the frustration of waiting for the EEOC to investigate harassment allegations only to find that the agency determined there was "no cause" for further action. Since all Title VII claims must travel through the EEOC for review and mediation, a complainant who sought assistance from federal civil rights law had to allow the agency 180 days to resolve her case. Women who waited out the 180 days could request "right to sue" letters even if their claims were still languishing at the EEOC, as could women whose claims reached some sort of conclusion. The expense of private legal counsel and litigation, however, often inhibited women from pursuing legal action. Also, again especially in hostile environment cases, the lack of monetary damages under Title VII before 1992 meant that there was little practical relief for a plaintiff even if she won her case (and no contingency fee for lawyers). Successful plaintiffs could recover damages under state discrimination laws or, in especially egregious cases, under state tort laws; but, again, the costs of litigating were daunting. All of these factors arguably deterred women from using sexual harassment law.

Added to the financial and legal hurdles to pursuing a harassment claim were the social costs of becoming a complainant. A woman who sought legal remedies exposed herself to harsh, even humiliating, treatment in court and risked being branded a troublemaker — or worse, a feminist — in the workplace.[12] Many women also hazarded

11. If a state or local Fair Employment Practices agency investigates a complaint first, the complainant has to file with the EEOC within thirty days of the FEP finding or within 300 days of the act of discrimination, whichever is earlier. Once the EEOC issues a "right-to-sue" letter, a complainant has ninety days to go to court. These deadlines apply to workers in nonfederal jobs. Federal workers have to follow different procedures and meet stricter time limits.

12. Naomi Wolf, "Feminism and Intimidation on the Job: Have the Hearings Liberated the Movement?" *Washington Post*, October 13, 1991.

being blacklisted by employers in their communities or by their professional networks.[13] The social costs of complaining about harassment thus could have severe economic repercussions.[14]

Faced with a complaint process that moved like molasses and a political process that wounded by impugning, many sexually harassed women chose silence rather than legal action, even after courts invited women to state their claims. Among the more famous examples of silenced women is Frances Conley, a Stanford University neurosurgeon, who stunned everyone in June 1991 by resigning her prestigious post because of sexual harassment. She had kept her harassment to herself for twenty-five years. By the time Anita Hill described the hostile environment Clarence Thomas had created for her, she had held her tongue for ten.

Anita Hill's riveting testimony raised consciousness of sexual harassment, though it did not improve the climate for women who try to do something about it. Her revelations educated America about how a supervisor can poison a woman's work environment by imposing unwelcome pornographic talk and sexual advances on her. They introduced the public to the concept of a hostile environment — and even disabused one senator of his assumption that sexual harassment requires touching.[15] But they did not convince majorities that Anita Hill had been harassed. A large majority (63 percent) believed that if Thomas actually had harassed Hill he should not be confirmed as a

13. Barbara Mathias, "The Harassment Hassle: Women Who Win Their Suits Sometimes Seem to Pay the Higher Price," *Washington Post*, October 20, 1991. Mathias tells the story of Pat Swanson, who lost her job when she rebuffed her boss's advances. During the two years it took her case to wend its way through the EEOC and to court, she was refused jobs — sometimes after receiving an initial offer.

14. Camille Hebert, "The Economic Implications of Sexual Harassment for Women," *Kansas Journal of Law & Public Policy*, vol. 3 (Spring 1994), 41–51.

15. "Committee's Handling of a Harassment Accusation Highlights Hidden Sex Issues," *New York Times*, October 8, 1991. Explaining why he hadn't considered Hill's story worth exploring when he first learned about it in September 1991, Senator Arlen Specter (R-Pennsylvania) said: "The lateness of the allegation, the absence of any touching or intimidation and the fact that she moved with him from one agency to another, I felt I had done my duty and was satisfied with his responses."

Supreme Court Justice — suggesting that a large majority considered harassment to be a serious matter. But a majority (55 percent) also believed that Thomas had *not* harassed Hill.[16] In the immediate wake of the hearings, only 29 percent of the public believed Hill's story: 27 percent of men and 31 percent of women; 28 percent of whites and 34 percent of people of color. Although more people found her credible with a year's hindsight (43 percent), a majority still expressed doubt.[17]

Hill's credibility collapsed beneath a barrage of assaults on her character. Under the influence of Thomas's friends C. Boyden Gray (then White House counsel), Dan Quayle (then vice president), and William Kristol (then Quayle's chief of staff), Republican aides strategized an attack on Hill's veracity, motives, and mental stability.[18] Senators Orrin Hatch, Arlen Specter, and Alan Simpson did the dirty work during the hearings themselves, along with witnesses who characterized Hill as delusional, vengeful, and ambitious.[19] Outside the committee room, seventeen women who had worked for Thomas sowed doubts about Hill's truthfulness in a press conference devoted to acquitting Thomas of "any improper behavior." They described Thomas as "sensitive," "almost puritanical," "chaste around the office," and "outrage[d] when he had even a whiff of impropriety on the part of any men in our agency." Moreover, one EEOC colleague asked, if Thomas really had harassed Hill, why was she complaining only *now?* "Had this occurred, the individual would have told someone . . . you don't sit back and be quiet for ten years."[20]

16. Richard Morin and Thomas Edsall, "More Americans Believe Thomas Than Accuser, Poll Indicates," *Washington Post*, October 13, 1991.

17. Leslie McAneny, "One Year Later: Anita Hill Now Deemed More Believable than Justice Thomas," *Gallup Poll Monthly*, October 1992, 35.

18. Andrew Rosenthal, "White House Role in Thomas Defense," *New York Times*, October 14, 1991; Maureen Dowd, "Republicans Gain in Battle by Getting Nasty Quickly," *New York Times*, October 15, 1991.

19. Caryl Rivers, "Is There No Believable Woman?" *Los Angeles Times*, December 12, 1991; Stanley Greenspan and Nancy Thorndike Greenspan, "Lies, Delusions and Truths: The Abuse of Psychiatry in the Thomas Hearings," *Washington Post*, October 29, 1991.

20. Barbara Vobejda, "No Evidence of Thomas Harassment, Nine Women Say: Former Education and EEOC Colleagues Turn Out to Support Supreme Court Nominee," *Washington Post*, October 11, 1991.

Her motives, morals, and mental state under fire from senators and citizens, Hill offered living, prime-time proof of the hostile political environment women who speak of their harassment must endure. As National Women's Law Center president Marcia Greenberger saw it, "the primary message is that if a woman comes forward, she is going to pay."[21] Compounding this discouraging lesson was that fact that only 31 percent of women believed Hill.[22]

Hill's treatment enraged leaders of feminist organizations and millions of feminists across the country. Far from dispirited either by the Senate's actions or by popular opinion, they seized the moment to revive public examination of how sexual imposition, humiliation, and predation rob women of agency, personhood, and equality.[23] They also vowed to make Congress more responsive to women's concerns, primarily by electing more women to serve there.[24] The face of Congress did change a little with the next election, when the number of women in the U.S. House of Representatives surged to forty-eight and when the number of women in the U.S. Senate tripled to six. Neither women's increased presence in Congress nor the heightened awareness of sexual harassment among the public have ended the political manhandling of women who tell of their harassment, however. Yet both did fuel major improvements in how the legal process treats sexually harassed plaintiffs. By 1999, some commenta-

21. E. J. Dionne Jr., "As Personal Becomes Political, Washington Gets an Education," *Washington Post*, October 15, 1991.

22. McAneny, "One Year Later," 35.

23. Cathleen Decker, "'We Believe You,' 900 Women Tell Anita Hill at Convention," *Los Angeles Times*, November 16, 1991.

24. Marjorie Williams, "The Feminist Roar, Heard Once More," *Washington Post*, October 11, 1991; Maralee Schwartz, "Feminists Vow to Seek Political Changes: Irked by Thomas Vote, Groups Plan to Put More Women in Congress," *Washington Post*, October 17, 1991; Judith Weinraub, "Women Have Sounded the Alarm for the Judiciary Committee 'Hit Man,'" *Washington Post*, October 18, 1991; Gwen Ifill, "Conference Lauds Anita Hill, Exultantly," *New York Times*, November 17, 1991; Kay Mills, "Harriet Woods: Thomas Hearings Jolted Women's Political Caucus Into Action," *Los Angeles Times*, December 1, 1991; Susan Carroll, *Women as Candidates in American Politics* (Bloomington, 1994), 159.

tors would blame these improvements for seeding a constitutional crisis that led to the impeachment of a president.[25]

NEW REMEDIES FOR SEX DISCRIMINATION

Clarence Thomas was confirmed to the Supreme Court on October 15, 1991. Ten days later, the Senate and the White House reached agreement on a civil rights measure that had been in dispute for nearly two years. Calling it a "quota bill," President Bush had vetoed the measure in 1990. Well into October 1991 he had flatly rejected provisions to make it harder for employers to justify business practices that yield discriminatory outcomes, arguing that such provisions would impel employers to adopt quotas for hiring and promotion to avoid lawsuits. Similarly, he had blocked unrestricted compensatory and punitive damages for intentional sex discrimination cases — including sexual harassment cases — asserting that a monetary remedy would "create a lawyers' bonanza" by encouraging frivolous lawsuits.[26] But in the white-hot aftermath of the Hill-Thomas controversy, Bush retracted his veto threats, relenting to pressures from Republican Senators who did not want to do further

25. E.g., Richard Dooling, "Making Criminals of Us All," *New York Times*, op-ed, December 30, 1998: "Were it not for the independent counsel statute and expanded interpretations of the sexual harassment laws, Mr. Starr would have had no authority to interrogate the President about his private sexual behavior. . . . Without these laws run amok, the scandal that has gripped the nation for the last year, and the constitutional crisis it created, would be the stuff of an Orwellian novel."

26. Helen Dewar, "Republican Warns Party on Opposing Rights Bill," *Washington Post*, October 24, 1991; Helen Dewar, "President Endorses Rights Compromise," *Washington Post*, October 26, 1991; Ruth Marcus, "Compromise on Civil Rights Bill Skirts Controversial Definition," *Washington Post*, October 26, 1991; Congresswoman Patsy Takemoto Mink (D-Hawaii), conversation with author, November 1, 1991. Mink was a member of the Education and Labor Committee, one of the two committees in the House of Representatives that handled the civil rights bill. The other committee was the Judiciary Committee.

battle on the terrain of sex and race.[27] Within weeks of Anita Hill's testimony, the Civil Rights Act of 1991 won strong majorities in Congress and by Thanksgiving was signed into law.[28]

The Act amended and strengthened Title VII by reversing a series of Supreme Court decisions handed down in 1989 that had made it more difficult to prove discrimination. Civil rights groups began lobbying aggressively for the legislation in 1989, when the Court gutted the disparate impact theory of discrimination in its decision in *Wards Cove Packing Co. v. Atonio.*[29] The decision stiffened requirements for stating a disparate impact claim, changed evidence standards, and made it easier for employers to defend themselves successfully. All of this made it very difficult for workers to win relief from formally neutral employer policies or practices that produce hiring, firing, or promotion outcomes skewed by race or by gender.

Disparate impact theory has been a pillar of Title VII adjudication since 1971, when the Court in *Griggs v. Duke Power Co.* ruled that formally race-neutral employment policies or practices — such as requiring a high school degree — may be discriminatory if they have the effect of disproportionately excluding minorities.[30] The Court extended disparate impact theory to sex discrimination in its 1977 decision in *Dothard v. Rawlinson.*[31] Under the theory, a 140-pound weight requirement for welders (for example) is actionable under Title VII if statistics show that such a requirement primarily weeds out women from this line of employment. An employer can escape Title VII liability by demonstrating that the requirement has

27. Michel McQueen and Jeffrey Birnbaum, "Thomas Battle, Duke's Rise in Louisiana Raised Stakes for Bush in Ending Civil Righs Impasse," *Wall Street Journal*, October 28, 1991; Ann Devroy, "Bush Saw Gains in Deal, Officials Say," *Washington Post*, October 26, 1991; Helen Dewar, "President Endorses Rights Compromise."

28. The Senate passed the bill by a vote of 93 to 5 and the House by a vote of 381 to 38. P.L. 102-166, 1991 WL 70454 (Leg. Hist.); http://thomas.loc.gov/cgi-bin/bdquery/z?d102:SN01745:@@@L|TOM:/bss/d102query, *Bill Summary and Status for the 102nd Congress*, S. 1745.

29. *Wards Cove Packing Co. v. Atonio*, 490 U.S. 642 (1989).

30. *Griggs v. Duke Power Co.*, 401 U.S. 424 (1971).

31. *Dothard v. Rawlinson*, 433 U.S. 321 (1977).

"a manifest relationship to the employment in question"—that it bears on the individual's job performance, thus serving a "business necessity."[32] Plaintiffs can rebut the employer's defense by establishing other means to meet the employer's objective. So, against an employer's claim that a weight requirement serves his business's need for strong workers, plaintiffs could argue that strength tests would be less discriminatory and would achieve the same objective.

Disparate impact theory examines the consequences of employer policies and practices, not how the policies and practices directly treat different groups of workers. The issue is not whether an employer intended to discriminate, but whether discrimination followed from its policies. Because the discriminatory consequences of employer practices are inferred from statistics, rather than from explicitly differential treatment, a disparate impact case looks at aggregates rather than individual circumstances, often is brought as a class action, and when successful provides relief to large groups of workers.

In contrast, an intentional discrimination case—where an employer allegedly takes an action "because of" sex or race—usually pivots on a showing of discriminatory motivation or purpose. Sexual harassment cases substitute a direct showing of intent with proof of unilateral discriminatory imposition, or unwelcomeness. Like disparate impact cases, all types of intentional discrimination cases seek to avenge discriminatory results. The results avenged must be caused by discriminatory actions or goals, however; they cannot be the unintended consequences of arguably benign practices.

Sometimes discriminatory action affects large numbers of workers, such as when an employer categorically excludes one race or sex. Categorical, or facial, discrimination—"whites only," "women need not apply"—deliberately excludes whole populations from employment opportunity. Intent is assumed, as the discrimination is explicitly stated in employment criteria; the criteria almost always violate Title VII. The only exception is in certain sex discrimination cases where an employer can prove that sex is a "bona fide occupational qualification."[33] When Title VII first became law, categorical sex-

32. *Griggs v. Duke Power Co.*
33. *UAW v. Johnson Controls, Inc.*, 499 U.S. 187, 201 (1991).

based exclusions from certain lines of work were not uncommon. Pan American Airways denied men employment as flight attendants, for example, while Alabama barred women from working as prison guards in maximum-security facilities.[34] This sort of discrimination is no longer typical — thanks in part to successful legal challenges by workers. If less conspicuous, discrimination nevertheless persists.

Over time, discrimination has become not only less official and more subtle, but also more individualized. Now rarely telegraphed in employer policies, discrimination often occurs one worker at a time, in decisions affecting particular job applicants or employees. Cases arising from this kind of discrimination — disparate treatment — are hard to prove absent witnesses or documents (or secret tapes) that can corroborate a plaintiff's claim that an employer is willfully biased. They are even harder to prove if the discrimination at issue can't be shown to be conscious or purposeful — if it is the product of assumptions or preferences that the employer has never articulated.

For workers who can identify employers' discriminatory acts, statements, or goals, the Supreme Court added a new hurdle to winning Title VII relief in 1989. In *Price Waterhouse v. Hopkins* the Court ruled that an employer could avoid liability for proven intentional discrimination if it could demonstrate at least one other motive for a challenged job action.[35] *Price Waterhouse* was a mixed-motive case in which the Court agreed with the plaintiff, Ann Hopkins, that sexual stereotyping had played a part in the firm's decision to deny her a partnership. Hopkins had been criticized by partners for being aggressive, abrasive, and "macho." The partner assigned to deliver the news that she would not be promoted advised her to "walk more femininely, talk more femininely, dress more femininely, wear makeup, have her hair styled, and wear jewelry."[36] Despite this proof of Price Waterhouse's sexist motivations, however, the Supreme Court did not hold the firm liable for sex discrimination. Instead, it invited the firm to show that it would have reached the same decision even if it had not taken Hopkins's gender transgressions into account.

34. *Diaz v. Pan American World Airways, Inc.*, 442 F. 2d 385 (5th Cir., 1971); *Dothard v. Rawlinson*, 433 U.S. 321 (1977).

35. *Price Waterhouse v. Hopkins*, 490 U.S. 228 (1989).

36. Ibid., at 1782.

If Price Waterhouse could show "by a preponderance of the evidence"—the lowest standard of proof—that it had other non-discriminatory reasons to deny Hopkins a partnership, then Hopkins would not be entitled to any relief at all.[37]

The Reagan-Bush administrations wanted to narrow Title VII to require proof of intent in all discrimination cases and to limit Title VII liability to those situations in which discrimination was the uniquely causal motivation for a disputed employment action. *Price Waterhouse* was one step in this direction. Preferring to approach discrimination on a case-by-case, individual-by-individual basis, the Republican administrations also wanted to reduce employers' liability for discrimination against whole classes of workers. *Wards Cove* accomplished just this.

The decision greatly disadvantaged workers, first by imposing stricter standards for establishing a prima facie case of disparate impact and then by giving employers more wiggle room when challenged. The decision applied a "specific causation" requirement to plaintiffs, under which they needed to isolate the precise employment practice that caused the race- or gender-based differential effect.[38] After *Wards Cove*, statistical evidence of race or gender imbalances in hiring or promotion would not be strong enough to create an inference of discrimination absent an empirically verifiable causal correlation with an employment practice. Institutional discrimination that results from congeries of assumptions, policies, and decisions would thus be difficult to contest. Plaintiffs who met the "specific causation" requirement were further disadvantaged by new rules of litigation that more closely tracked disparate treatment cases. Disparate treatment defendants have to show a "legitimate" nondiscriminatory reason for the disputed action.[39] Under *Griggs*, disparate impact defendants had to establish the relevance of disputed practices to job performance and "business necessity." *Wards Cove* ended this tougher test ("there is no requirement that the challenged practice be 'essential' or 'indispensable' to the employer's business for it to pass muster"), asking employers only to state a vaguer "legitimate

37. Ibid., at 1795.
38. *Wards Cove Packing Co. v. Atonio*, at 657–58.
39. *Texas Dept. of Community Affairs v. Burdine*, 450 U.S. 248 (1981).

business justification" for the practices at issue.[40] Further, *Wards Cove* made it the responsibility of plaintiffs to *dis*prove the employer's defense.[41]

In the Civil Rights Act of 1991, Congress corrected *Wards Cove*, *Price Waterhouse*, and five other Supreme Court decisions that undermined civil rights law.[42] In an unusual instance of legislative specificity, Congress "codified *Griggs*," effectively directing the Supreme Court to restore most of what *Wards Cove* had destroyed. A section of the act entitled "Burden of Proof in Disparate Impact Cases" revived the "job-relatedness" and "business necessity" standards, requiring employers to prove that suspect practices meet the standards.[43] Although the act did not overturn the "specific causation" requirement of *Wards Cove*, it added mitigating language that permits a plaintiff to challenge an employer's decision-making process as a whole if she can show that the elements of the process "are incapable of separation for analysis."[44]

Additionally, the act modified the *Price Waterhouse* rule allowing employers in mixed-motive cases to escape liability even when discrimination was proved. The act clarified that employment discrimination always is illegal and must be remedied under Title VII. A plaintiff who shows discrimination is entitled to injunctive relief, as well as to attorneys' fees, even if other factors also account for the employment decision she's challenging. The act also relaxed the

40. *Wards Cove Packing Co. v. Atonio*, at 659.

41. Ibid., at 659–660.

42. *Patterson v. McLean Credit Union*, 491 U.S. 164 (1989), ending protections under Section 1981 of the Civil Rights Act of 1866 for discrimination on the job by confining coverage to hiring; *Martin v. Wilks*, 490 U.S. 755 (1989), permitting white firefighters in Birmingham, Alabama, to challenge a court-approved consent decree; *Lorance v. AT&T*, 490 U.S. 900 (1989), requiring workers to contest a discriminatory seniority rule at the time it is adopted, not when they are adversely affected by it; *Equal Employment Opportunity Commission v. Aramco*, 499 U.S. 244 (1991), relieving U.S. companies abroad from Title VII compliance; *West Virginia University Hospitals v. Casey*, 499 U.S. 83 (1991), ruling that the costs of expert witnesses could not be considered part of the attorneys' fees to which a successful plaintiff was entitled.

43. P.L. 102-166, Section 105.

44. Ibid.

statute of limitations for federal workers in Title VII actions from thirty days to ninety days (still a shorter period than the 180 days for nonfederal employees). And, in an obvious but begrudging bow to Anita Hill and the women she mobilized, the Senate set up an office to field its own staff's complaints of sexual harassment.[45]

If the first purpose of the 1991 Civil Rights Act was to direct the adjudication of civil rights claims, providing monetary remedies for targets of intentional discrimination was its second. It was also a second battlefront for the Bush White House and the Democratic Congress. Democratic civil rights bills sought to expand Title VII remedies to include monetary relief for the personal injuries of intentional discrimination. (Title VII remedies under the 1964 Civil Rights Act were limited to equitable relief — back pay, job reinstatement, or an injunction against further discrimination.) The bill that President Bush vetoed in 1990 would have permitted successful plaintiffs to recover full compensatory damages, as well as punitive damages up to $150,000 or the amount of the compensatory damage award, whichever was greater.[46] H.R. 1, the Democratic House bill under consideration in 1991, would not have imposed any limits on punitive damages. Compensatory damages could be claimed for humiliation, pain and suffering, medical expenses, and other out-of-pocket costs. Punitive damages could be awarded against employers who discriminated with malice or with reckless indifference to workers' civil rights.

Congressional Republicans sought to cap damages at $100,000 and to limit awards to those plaintiffs who could not collect back pay and even then only when judges determined that an award was necessary to deter future discrimination by the employer. In his message accompanying his veto of the 1990 civil rights bill, President Bush echoed congressional Republicans in denouncing the bill for creating a new tort remedy and for "radically alter[ing] the remedial pro-

45. Gwen Ifill, "Capitalizing on the Thomas Fallout," *New York Times*, October 28, 1991; Judy Mann, "Feminism, Alive and Well," *Washington Post*, November 1, 1991.

46. U.S. House of Representatives, H.R. 4000, *Civil Rights Act of 1990*, 101st Congress, 2nd Session; U.S. House of Representatives, H.R. 1, *Civil Rights and Women's Equity in Employment Act of 1991*, Section 206.

vision of Title VII of the Civil Rights Act of 1964."[47] He went on to call for an "equitable monetary award" in sexual harassment cases only, to be capped at $150,000 and to be awarded by judges when necessary to deter future violations.[48] Deep into fall 1991, Democrats and Republicans were at a standoff on this issue.

The authors and proponents of civil rights legislation proposed the damages remedy for intentional discrimination for at least two reasons. First, without damages available under Title VII, federal civil rights law treated race and sex discrimination in employment differently. Plaintiffs successful in intentional race discrimination cases were entitled to unrestricted damages under a 1975 application of a Reconstruction Era civil rights measure.[49] Section 1981 of the Civil Rights Act of 1866 forbids race discrimination in making and enforcing private contracts, including employment, and authorizes both equitable relief and monetary damages for race discrimination plaintiffs. Intentional race discrimination plaintiffs in Title VII cases can avail themselves of a Section 1981 claim and, if successful, can win compensatory and punitive monetary awards. Hence, although the damages amendment to Title VII covered all intentional employment discrimination prohibited under the Civil Rights Act of 1964, it would improve remedies available to plaintiffs especially in nonrace cases — primarily women.

Some women also have been able to recover damages for sex discrimination in employment under 19th century civil rights law, but only when the perpetrator is a state government or public official and only when Title VII does not apply. Section 1983 (originally Section 1 of the Ku Klux Klan Act of 1871) holds states and persons acting under color of state law liable for deprivations of rights "secured

47. *Congressional Record*, October 22, 1990, p. S16418.

48. U.S. House of Representatives, Committee on Education and Labor, *Memorandum Re: Wednesday, February 27, 1991 Hearing on H.R. 1: The Civil Rights Act of 1991*, 102nd Congress, 1st Session, February 26, 1991 (author's files).

49. 42 U.S.C. Section 1981. In 1975, the Supreme Court held that Section 1981 provides a full federal damages remedy against race discrimination in private employment. *Johnson v. Railway Express Agency, Inc.*, 421 U.S. 454 (1975).

by the Constitution and laws" and authorizes appropriate remedies.[50] Once the Supreme Court determined that the Fourteenth Amendment prohibits sex and gender discrimination,[51] Section 1983 became a tool for enforcing employment rights for women who are state or local employees. However, many courts do not permit plaintiffs to use Section 1983 if that would duplicate a Title VII claim. Thus, Section 1983 is a tool usually restricted to employment plaintiffs who can show that their constitutional rights have been violated. Even so, it is a significant alternative for state employees like Paula Jones who seek redress directly from their harassers, for Section 1983 holds individuals liable for infringing rights.[52]

One reason to make compensatory and punitive damages available under Title VII was to make the same remedies available to intentional discrimination targets regardless of the type of discrimination they endure. A second reason was to extend to sex discrimination targets remedies that are appropriate to their circumstances. Sex discrimination plaintiffs explained the inadequacy of existing Title VII remedies at congressional hearings, and committee reports were jammed with examples of women who had been ill served by civil rights law.

One woman, Nancy Phillips, was fired after she told her employer that she was pregnant. Not only did she lose her source of income, but also her family's health insurance. The hospital where she delivered her baby sued her when she couldn't pay the bills and threatened to send a marshal to her home to collect the judgment. By the time

50. 42 U.S.C. Section 1983.

51. While sex and gender discrimination violate the equal protection clause, not all sex or gender classifications are considered discriminatory. The Court requires such classifications to be "substantially related" to "important governmental objectives" to pass constitutional muster. Those that do are permissible, i.e., not discriminatory. *Craig v. Boren*, 429 U.S. 190 (1976).

52. Cheryl L. Anderson, "'Nothing Personal': Individual Liability Under 42 U.S.C. Section 1983 for Sexual Harassment as an Equal Protection Claim," *Berkeley Journal of Employment and Labor Law* 19 (1998): 60–107; George Likourezos, "Sexual Harassment by a Public Official Gives Rise to a Section 1983 Claim: A Legal Argument," *Women's Rights Law Reporter* 15 (Winter/Spring 1993–94): 159–168.

a court held her employer liable for sex discrimination, her family was deeply in debt. Under Title VII, she could recover back pay and pregnancy-related medical expenses, but nothing to compensate for the stress, humiliation, or financial strain precipitated by the discrimination.

Another woman, a physical education teacher, filed a Title VII claim against her employer for discriminatory working conditions. She had been forced to share her students' toilet and shower facilities and to use a partitioned space within the girls' locker room as her office — while her male colleagues enjoyed their own offices, as well as private toilets, lockers, and showers. Although a court ruled in her favor, she didn't receive any relief or compensation for the discrimination: she had suffered no wage injury, so back pay was not appropriate; and because she had retired by the time she won her case, the court decided an injunction against the discrimination was not relevant either.[53]

The most glaring and most numerous examples of discrimination that could not be put right under Title VII involved sexual harassment targets. Committee reports accompanying various drafts of the civil rights bill summarized a string of court cases in which women who had won verdicts against their harassers could not win back what they had lost in time, occupational standing, social acceptance, equanimity, or health — not to mention associated economic costs. They also recorded testimony from sexually harassed women.

Appearing before the House Committee on Education and Labor, Jacqueline Morris described the regimen of sexual humiliation she had had to endure for years. At the glass bottle manufacturing plant where she was a machinist, Morris's supervisors had touched her breasts and buttocks and had offered vulgar and intrusive speculations about her sexual practices. Her co-workers littered her work station with a pair of women's underwear, a soiled sanitary napkin, a

53. These and other women's stories are summarized in U.S. House of Representatives, Committee on Education and Labor, House Report No. 102–40 (I), *The Civil Rights and Women's Equity in Employment Act of 1991*, 102nd Congress, 1st Session, April 24, 1991; Committee on the Judiciary, House Report No. 102-40 (II), *The Civil Rights Act of 1991*, 102nd Congress, 1st Session, May 17, 1991.

clay replica of a penis, a sausage with a note that said "bite me baby," and other offensive materials. At one point, she was asked, "Do you spit or swallow?" After she filed a complaint with the EEOC, the harassment escalated. She began to suffer nervousness, sleeplessness, blotches and welts on her legs and back, and difficulty breathing; she also began to miss work. The company's doctor concluded that Morris's health problems were a result of the harassment and told her that she would have a nervous breakdown if she did not quit. She left the company, but returned a year later. Unable to find another job as a machinist, she had been forced to take a $10.21 pay cut and work as a waitress for $2.65 an hour. She couldn't meet her mortgage and car payments earning only $2.65 an hour, so she went back to the bottle factory. Morris nonetheless persisted with her case against her employer. A federal judge ruled in her favor, holding the company liable for at least two and a half years of sexual harassment. But all she recovered under Title VII was $16,000 in back pay — a fraction of her actual wage loss. She received nothing for the physical and psychic toll of the harassment or for related expenses.[54]

In a statement submitted to the House Education and Labor Commitee, Lois Robinson told a similar story. Robinson was a welder at a Florida shipyard. Over a period of years, her co-workers taunted her with pornographic materials such as a dart board with a woman's nipple as the bull's eye; with demeaning graffiti such as "lick me you whore dog bitch"; and with degrading comments such as "I'd like to get in bed with that." Robinson lost sleep, suffered neck pain and nausea, and sometimes skipped work because she could not face what awaited her there. When her employer would not respond to her complaints, she turned to the EEOC and the courts. A federal district court found that she had been subject to a hostile environment for which her employer was liable under Title VII. The court did not award Robinson any of the $13,600 she had lost in pay as a result of missed work, however, because she could not establish precisely

54. "Statement of Jacqueline Morris Before the Committee on Education and Labor, United States House of Representatives," February 27, 1991 (author's files); *Morris v. American Nat'l Can Co.*, 730 F. Supp. at 1490-91 (E.D. Missouri, 1989).

which days she had missed due to harassment. As a surrogate for back pay, the court granted her $1.00 in nominal damages — vindicating her in principle but without relieving her misery.[55]

Without a possibility of restitution under Title VII, Jacqueline Morris, Lois Robinson, and countless other women bore the non-wage costs of the sexual harassment inflicted on them. Not only was this unfair to sexual harassment plaintiffs, it also discouraged many sexually harassed women from coming forward at all. As one judge put it, "There is little incentive for a plaintiff to bring a Title VII suit when the best that she can hope for is an order to her supervisor and to her employer to treat her with the dignity she deserves and the costs of bringing her suit."[56]

Feminist legal advocates — the National Women's Law Center and the Women's Legal Defense Fund, for example — and their congressional allies argued that this undermined the aim of Title VII, which is to end practices that create or perpetuate inequality in the workplace. While no one pretended that monetary damages could restore all that a plaintiff might have lost from discrimination, proponents insisted that damages were necessary to provide plaintiffs a modicum of relief — and an incentive to come forward. Moreover, they maintained that full compensatory and punitive damages would give employers incentive to prevent and stop sexual harassment and other forms of sex discrimination.

Opponents argued that a damages remedy would open the floodgates to frivolous lawsuits, expose employers to prohibitive awards, and scuttle Title VII's mechanisms for mediation and voluntary settlement. Proponents countered with evidence from race cases under Section 1981, which permits monetary awards. According to a House Committee on Education and Labor report, decisions were reported in only 594 Section 1981 cases during the decade between 1980 and 1990. Of those, compensatory or punitive damages were awarded in only sixty-nine. Two-thirds of the awards were for $50,000 or less,

55. "Statement of Lois Robinson, Hearing on the Civil Rights Act of 1991, H.R. 1, House Committee on Education and Labor," February 27, 1991 (author's files).

56. *Mitchell v. OsAir*, 629 F. Supp. 636, 643 (N.D. Ohio, E.D., 1986).

and in only four cases did the award exceed $200,000.[57] Further, proponents argued that despite the lure of unrestricted damages, intentional race discrimination complainants routinely used the Title VII conciliation process, accepting settlements at rates comparable to their sex discrimination counterparts.[58]

The Hill-Thomas controversy jump-started negotiations on a final civil rights bill that accomplished many of the objectives of its civil rights and feminist proponents. Still, the Civil Rights Act of 1991 was a product of compromise. For example, a "specific causation" requirement was retained for disparate impact cases, though it was less stringent than the one originally announced by the Supreme Court and supported by the Bush Administration. Also, while the act was quite precise about the structure of adjudication under Title VII, it nowhere defined the "business necessity" test in disparate impact cases. And although the act does provide injunctive relief to a winning plaintiff in a mixed-motive case, it deprives her of monetary relief if her employer can show it would have made the same adverse decision without the discrimination.[59]

Compromise was even more pronounced on the damages issue. President Bush and congressional Republicans urged setting a low ceiling on monetary awards and specifying narrow circumstances under which judges alone could grant awards. Congressional Democrats, with their allies in the civil rights and feminist communities, favored unrestricted damages to be decided by juries. In the end, Democrats lost their bid for full damages but won a damages provision; Republicans lost their case for extremely low damage limits but won a capped and graduated damages scheme; and workers won the right to jury trials when they seek damages. Under the new Section 1981A, intentional discrimination plaintiffs can recover up to $50,000 from employers with 15 to 100 employees; $100,000 from employers with 101 to 200 employees; $200,000 from employers with 201 to 500 employees; and $300,000 from employers with more than

57. House Report No. 102-40 (I) at notes 68 and 69; *Memorandum Re: Wednesday, February 27, 1991 Hearing on H.R. 1.*
58. House Report No. 102-40 (I) at note 70.
59. P.L. 102-166, Section 107.

500 employees.[60] Most employers have fewer than 100 employees, so most women live under the $50,000 cap on Title VII damages — regardless of how malicious, reckless, or egregious the discrimination against them.

Viewing the damages provision as a second-class remedy for women, feminist groups were unhappy with the civil rights compromise. Brokered by the Republican White House and Senators John Danforth (R-Missouri) and Edward Kennedy (D-Massachusetts), the compromise involved significant concessions by Republicans on the disparate impact issue and a signal concession by Democrats on women's civil rights remedies. The Senate Democrats' decision to meet President Bush halfway on women's remedies was especially vexing in the wake of the Hill-Thomas hearings. The hearings had been convened only after feminists in the House of Representatives, national feminist organizations, and tens of thousands of women across the country had hounded the Senate into convening them. On first learning of Anita Hill's experience from committee investigators, the Judiciary Committee — chaired by Senator Joseph Biden (D-Delaware)— had ducked the issue. Even after the story broke publicly, the Judiciary Committee and then-Senate Majority Leader George Mitchell had resisted taking it seriously.[61] When the Judiciary Committee finally heard Hill's testimony, it revealed bipartisan ignorance about sexual harassment, insensitivity to the circumstances of harassed women, and fierce suspicion of any woman willing to talk

60. The damages provision was codified in 42 U.S.C. Section 1981A.

61. When news of Hill's allegations first leaked, leaders of feminist organizations and prominent feminist legal advocates lobbied Senate Majority Leader George Mitchell to delay the vote on Thomas's confirmation until the matter could be investigated. He refused, saying, "My hands are tied." After denouncing the Senate's plans for business as usual from the House floor, a group of feminist congresswomen marched to the Senate Majority Leader's office to demand a delay in the confirmation vote. He told them to lobby Democratic Senators who had announced support for Thomas. Later that day, he negotiated a delay in the vote with Minority Leader Bob Dole (R-Kansas) and Thomas's shepherd, Senator Danforth. Mayer and Abramson, *Strange Justice*, 268–270; and conversation with Congresswoman Patsy Takemoto Mink (D-Hawaii), who participated in the struggle to win a hearing for Hill.

about it. Needless to say, the 99 percent male Senate's decision to cap damages and peg the caps to the size of a plaintiff's employer was received as another slap at women — another sign that, in the catchphrase of the day, "they just don't get it."[62]

Nonetheless, most feminist groups ultimately accepted the damages provision as a first step and deferred a fight for unrestricted damages to another day.[63] There was good reason to believe that another day would come. Two days before voting on the civil rights bill, the Senate passed a resolution "Condemning Sexual Harassment," for example.[64] Further, during the floor debate on the civil rights bill, numerous Senators professed deep concern for the problem of sexual harassment, decrying arbitrary damage caps even as they accepted the compromise. Making good on promises to try to undo the caps in separate legislation, Senator Kennedy introduced the Equal Remedies Act with thirty cosponsors on November 26, 1991.[65]

Another day hasn't come yet; monetary remedies against sex discrimination in employment continue to be restricted. Still, the availability of any damages at all means that some women who might not have come forward before do come forward now.

During the Hill-Thomas hearings, many Senators wondered out loud why Hill—who must have been an expert on Title VII as a lawyer for the EEOC—never sought protection from the law. But the protections available to her under Title VII were not responsive

62. Congresswoman Mink, conversations with author.

63. Judith Lichtman and Holly Fechner, "Almost There," *Human Rights* 19 (Summer 1992): 16–19.

64. S. Res. 209, *Condemning Sexual Harassment*, 1991 WL 220131 (Cong. Rec.).

65. *Congressional Record*, Wednesday, October 30, 1991, e.g., S15482 (Gore, D-Tennessee), S15488 (Kennedy, D-Massachusetts), S15489 (Leahy, D-Vermont), S15490 (Durenberger, R-Minnesota), S15493 (Kerry, D-Massachusetts), S15494 (Riegle, D-Michigan), S15495 (Dixon, D-Illinois), S15496 (Akaka, D-Hawaii), S15497 (Wellstone, D-Minnesota). Representative Barbara Kennelly (D-Connecticut) introduced the House companion to S. 2062, The Equal Remedies Act, on November 26, 1991, with fifty cosponsors (that number would grow to 117 by mid-1992). Neither the Senate nor the House bill became law.

to the harms of harassment and not even suitable to a target's circumstances. Had she taken her case to court, Hill might have won an injunction against further harassment. However, injunctions are not easily enforceable against much of the interpersonal conduct that is sexual harassment; they also often precipitate subtle retaliation or more intense hostility from perpetrators.[66] Had Hill quit her job because of the harassment she might have been entitled to back pay. She would have had to prove, however, that she had been "constructively discharged"—that is, that she had been compelled to resign as a direct consequence of the harassment.[67] She also might have won reinstatement. Returning to work alongside her harasser, however, would not have been a viable option had she left her job because of the unbearable strain of being around him.

The Civil Rights Act of 1991 fashioned more appropriate remedies, so someone like Hill might now consider using the law to resist her harassment—might risk the social consequences of speaking up to win some restitution. Indeed, many more women do seem willing to take just such a risk. The number of sexual harassment complaints filed with the EEOC jumped between 1991 and 1998, from 6,883 in FY1991 to 15,889 in FY1997.

Correspondingly, the monetary settlements secured through EEOC grievance and resolution processes rose from $7.1 million in FY1991 to $49.5 million in FY1997 (not including awards and settlements won in litigation).[68] This reflects not only the increase in the number of complainants but also the pressures of potential jury awards. With damages available, the price tag for sexual harassment could be staggering, at least in cases where large numbers of women in large firms are subject to a hostile environment. In 1997, for example, Mitsubishi Motor Manufacturing of America agreed to a

66. Jane E. Larson and Jonathan A. Knee, "We *Can* Do Something About Sexual Harassment," *Washington Post*, October 22, 1991.

67. This requires proof of harassment that is more severe and more pervasive than is necessary to prove a hostile working environment. *American Jurisprudence*, 2d ed., vol. 45B (1993), Sections 954 and 968.

68. http://www.eeoc.gov/stats/harass.html, Equal Employment Opportunity Commission, *Sexual Harassment Charges: EEOC & FEPAs Combined, FY1991–FY1997*.

$9.5 million settlement with twenty-seven women employees who had complained of sexual harassment. In 1998, the company entered a consent decree with the EEOC under which it will pay $34 million to some 350 women who had been subject to sexual harassment at its plant in Normal, Illinois.[69]

Sexual harassment targets now are credible threats to employers' profits. This obviously gives employers incentive to respond effectively when sexual harassment occurs and to enforce policies to prevent it in the first place. But it also gives employers and other skeptics incentive to trash targets who claim monetary relief for sexual harassment as being "just in it for the money."

NEW GROUND RULES FOR DEFENDANTS

The 1991 Civil Rights Act improved remedies available to successful plaintiffs but did little to mitigate the risks of pressing a sexual harassment claim. It did not protect targets from being blamed for their own harassment, ostracized at work or in the community, or blacklisted on the job market. It did not defend them from revelations about their intimate lives or speculations about their mental health. Worst of all, it did not shield them from the inconsolable pain of not being believed.

Nevertheless, Anita Hill's personal courage inspired many women to report harassment incidents. In the immediate aftermath of the Hill-Thomas hearings, some women emulated Hill by telling their stories publicly at speak-outs across the country. Others were emboldened to take formal action against powerful institutions and individuals: Lieutenant Paula Coughlin, for example, mauled sexually at the 1991 Tailhook convention, publicly filed an official complaint with the U.S. Navy in June, 1992;[70] a few months later, ten women revealed that they had been sexually harassed by Senator Bob Packwood

69. *Equal Employment Opportunity Commission v. Mitsubishi Motor Manufacturing of America*, Joint Motion for Entry of Consent Decree, Case No. 96-1192 (C.D. Ill., 1998).

70. Jean Zimmerman, *Tailspin: Women at War in the Wake of Tailhook* (New York, 1995), 90–92.

(R-Oregon).[71] These disclosures radically increased public awareness of sexual harassment and nourished a professed public consensus that harassment is unacceptable. Backed up by more suitable remedies at law, these political developments encouraged more women to gamble on winning justice. In the two years following adoption of the 1991 Civil Rights Act, the number of sexual harassment charges filed with the EEOC nearly doubled.[72] By 1993, sexual harassment complainants were seeking right to sue letters in 24.4 percent of all EEOC cases, up from 13.3 percent in 1990.[73]

Still, the vast majority of sexually harassed women continued to keep their silence. Even so, any increase at all in the number of plaintiffs heightened employers' litigation costs. Damages compounded those costs with the rising price of liability. Employers responded by sharpening their knives for character assassination. As the plaintiff's attorney in a sexual harassment lawsuit against a Chicago law firm explained, "They want to prove [she] is a nut or a slut."[74]

This was not a new tactic. Defendants in sexual harassment cases long had assailed their accusers' characters — or had blackmailed them into silence by threatening to do so. But as the stakes of sexual harassment cases increased with the addition of jury awards, so too did defendants' inquiries into their accusers' sexual relationships, behaviors, and practices. Many courts treated such inquiries as fair game — as an element of a complete defense — against a harassment target's claim that the defendant's conduct had been unwelcome or offensive. Observing that "companies are fighting back with every legal weapon at hand," the *Wall Street Journal* quoted one defense attorney's strategy: "If the plaintiff talked about sex on the job, it

71. Florence Graves and Charles E. Shepard, "Packwood Accused of Sexual Advances: Alleged Behavior Pattern Counters Image," *Washington Post*, November 22, 1992.

72. *Sexual Harassment Charges: EEOC & FEPAs Combined: FY1991–FY1997.*

73. Paul Nicholas Monnin, "Proving Welcomeness: The Admissibility of Evidence of Sexual History in Sexual Harassment Claims Under the 1994 Amendments to Federal Rule of Evidence 412," *Vanderbilt Law Review* 48 (May 1995): n. 6.

74. Ellen E. Schultz and Junda Woo, "The Bedroom Ploy," *Wall Street Journal*, September 19, 1994.

makes inquiries into her sexual background relevant. . . . If she claims the harassment interfered with her sex life, her extramarital affairs become relevant."[75] As a side benefit, even when evidence about a woman's sex life was not dispositive, it could infect a jury with prejudice against her.[76]

Defendants did not have untrammeled discretion, however. Litigation rules bar the use of evidence to show "propensity." In sexual harassment cases, the propensity rule means that defendants can't introduce character evidence to establish that a woman tended to want sex, act sexual, or invite sexual attention — and therefore must have welcomed it from her harasser.[77] But the very Supreme Court decision that confirmed sexual harassment's place in the framework of discrimination law also created a loophole through which defendants could marshal nonpropensity character evidence that can discredit a woman's claim.

In *Meritor Savings Bank v. Vinson*, the Court held that an alleged harasser's conduct must be judged by whether it was welcomed. It further asserted that courts must ascertain "whether respondent *by her conduct* indicated that the alleged sexual advances were unwelcome."[78] According to the Court, evidence about a plaintiff's attire, speech, or fantasies might be relevant to a welcomeness inquiry. Courts thus must look to "the totality of the circumstances" and "the record as a whole" to gauge whether sexual harassment has occurred.[79]

The unwelcomeness standard invites a defendant to turn a plaintiff's capacity for offense into a threshold question, as if a woman who isn't offended by behavior necessarily welcomes it.[80] It also gives a defendant license to introduce evidence of a plaintiff's sexually provocative behavior. Searching for signs of participation to establish welcomeness, many courts have required that this sort of character evidence pertain to a plaintiff's conduct with or around an al-

75. Ibid.

76. Monnin, "Proving Welcomeness," 1187, n. 110; Susan Estrich, "Sex at Work," *Stanford Law Review* 43 (1991): 827–830.

77. Federal Rules of Evidence 404(a).

78. *Meritor Savings Bank v. Vinson*, 477 U.S. 57, 68 (1986) [my italics].

79. Ibid.

80. Monnin, "Proving Welcomeness."

leged harasser. Some courts have required that the evidence be strongly connected to the alleged harassment, not merely be suggestive of a target's receptivity to a perpetrator's attentions.[81] That said, the *Meritor* formula grants broad latitude to a defendant to seek information about a plaintiff. One defendant, for example, introduced evidence that the plaintiff had once posed nude for a national magazine to prove that she couldn't have been offended by his conduct. The district court agreed.[82]

Obviously, if deciding whether harassment has occurred can depend on first deciding whether a woman is vulnerable to injury from a man's sexual conduct, then the social costs of complaining about harassment can be quite high. In the face of further degradation and violation, few harassment targets take formal action against their perpetrators. Hence, although the introduction of jury awards gave women incentive to use the law, the prerogatives of defendants in the discovery and trial process gave women countervailing incentive not to do so.

In the Violence Against Women Act of 1994 (VAWA), Congress mitigated this imbalance between plaintiffs' rights and defendants' prerogatives in civil sex offense cases, including sexual harassment cases, that arise under federal laws. Extending the logic of the criminal rape shield it had enacted in 1978, Congress in 1994 restricted the use of evidence about a plaintiff's sexual behavior, predisposition, or reputation in civil sex offense cases.[83] An amendment to Federal Rule of Evidence 412, the civil shield declares evidence about a target's sex life is "generally inadmissible," as it is under the criminal rape shield (the original evidence rule 412).[84] Reputation evidence is admissible in civil cases — where it is not under the criminal rape shield — but only if a target has placed her reputation in contro-

81. E.g., *Wangler v. Hawaiian Electric Co., Inc.*, 742 F. Supp. 1458-64 (D. Hawaii, 1990).

82. *Burns v. McGregor Electronic Industries, Inc.*, 807 F. Supp. 506 (N.D. Iowa, 1992).

83. H.R. 3355, *The Violent Crime Control and Law Enforcement Act of 1994*, Title IV, *The Violence Against Women Act*, Chapter 4, "New Evidentiary Rules," Section 40141. Codified as amended Federal Rule of Evidence 412.

84. F.R.E. 412 (a).

versy.[85] A civil defendant may ask a court to admit evidence that is "otherwise admissible" under the federal rules of evidence, but to prevail would have to refer to specific acts and show that the probative value of the evidence "substantially outweighs the danger of harm to any victim and of unfair prejudice to any party."[86]

The rape shield provision of evidence rule 412 had been an important feminist achievement — testimony to the influence of organized feminism in the 1970s, to the vigor of grassroots mobilizations against sexualized violence, as well as to the resolve of feminists in Congress.[87] So too was the extension of the shield to civil cases. As a provision of the Violence Against Women Act, the civil sex offense shield was a core element of one of two major feminist legislative victories following the 1992 return of Democrats to the White House and the election of unprecedented numbers of women to the Congress (the other major legislative victory being the Family and Medical Leave Act). Importantly, the act's legislative history specifically linked the civil sex offense shield to the vindication of women's rights. According to the conference report accompanying the act, in addition to safeguarding a plaintiff against embarrassment, sexual stereotyping, and privacy invasions, "the rule also encourages victims of sexual misconduct to institute and to participate in legal proceedings against alleged offenders." Moreover, the Notes of the Advisory Committee of the Judicial Conference of the United States, adopted in the congressional conference report, explicitly stated that "Rule 412 will . . . apply in a Title VII action in which the plaintiff has alleged sexual harassment."[88]

While the criminal rape shield established a critical principle in federal criminal law and offered a model to states that had not yet

85. F.R.E. 412 (b) (2).

86. Ibid.

87. Congresswoman Elizabeth Holtzman (D-New York) was the chief sponsor of the federal criminal rape shield, H.R. 4727, which became law in 1978.

88. U.S. House of Representatives, Judicial Conference Advisory Committee Notes on Evidence Rule 412, Conference Report No. 103-711, 103rd Congress, 2d Session (1994). See also, Julie A. Springer, Phyllis Pollard, and R. Paige Arnette, "Survey of Selected Evidentiary Issues in Employment Law," *Baylor Law Review* 50 (Spring 1998): 428–435.

considered such a modification to state evidence rules, it did not protect most raped women in the prosecution of their rapists. The federal rape shield applies only to rape prosecutions in federal courts; meanwhile, most rapes are prosecuted under state, not federal, law. The civil sex offense shield, by contrast, covers all raped, sexually assaulted, or sexually harassed women (or men) when they seek remedies under federal civil rights laws.

When Congress amended Rule 412 to cover plaintiffs in civil sex offense cases, it destabilized the *Meritor* framework. For that reason, the Supreme Court objected to the amended rule. In an oddly pro-defendant letter to the Judicial Conference, Chief Justice Rehnquist explained, "[t]his Court recognized in *Meritor Savings Bank v. Vinson* . . . that evidence of an alleged victim's 'sexually provocative speech or dress' may be relevant in workplace harassment cases, and some Justices expressed concern that the proposed amendment might encroach on the rights of defendants."[89] Notwithstanding the Court's worry, the civil shield does not provide hermetic protection to sexual harassment plaintiffs. Not a few courts have permitted defendants to explore plaintiffs' sexual conduct and history, at least in the workplace, if their past behavior arguably is germane to the harassment charge or to its defense.[90] Many courts do draw the line at a plaintiff's private life — her conduct and relationships outside the workplace — but only so long as she does not put her private life into question.[91]

It's not an easy line to hold, however, since many of the injuries of harassment are deeply personal. Many plaintiffs point to emotional distress, fear, shame, and other psychic injuries to show that their harassers' conduct was offensive. Evidence rule 412 does not prevent a defendant from searching for information to disprove a plaintiff's capacity for offense if a judge considers such information more proba-

89. Quoted in Monnin, "Proving Welcomeness," n. 122.

90. E.g., *Sanchez v. Zabihi, et al.*, 166 F.R.D. 500 (D. New Mexico, 1996), holding that because the employer's defense was that the plaintiff was the sexual aggressor, the employer could inquire into her past history of making sexual or romantic advances toward other employees.

91. E.g., *Delaney v. City of Hampton, Virginia*, 999 F. Supp. 794 (E.D. Virginia, 1997), finding evidence of the plaintiff's past sexual abuse to be admissible so that the employer could prove that her psychiatric condition was caused by stress other than alleged sexual abuse by a co-worker.

tive than prejudicial and likely to lead to admissible evidence. President Clinton, for example, investigated Paula Jones's sex life, taking depositions from "other men" to suggest that she could not have been harmed by the president's proposition. Although the president denied Jones's charges, he also sought to rebut them by showing that she had engaged in prior acts of casual oral sex. According to a brief he filed on January 7, 1998, prior acts evidence would prove that Paula Jones was not "an innocent minister's daughter, or . . . unfamiliar with oral sex, or . . . emotionally traumatized by a suggestion that she perform oral sex."[92]

The main effect of the civil sex offense shield is to shift the burden to the defendant to convince the court that the evidence he seeks is probative, or more likely to prove a fact, than it is prejudicial. Moreover, the civil shield affords plaintiffs certain procedural safeguards, such as protective orders governing the scope of discovery or guarding the confidentiality of personal evidence. Thus, although the shield does not eliminate the *Meritor* court's behavioral test for unwelcomeness or shut the door to a defendant's behavioral rebuttal to an offensiveness claim, it does set some boundaries for defendants and thereby attenuates some of the risks plaintiffs face.

President Clinton signed the Violence Against Women Act into law on September 13, 1994, as part of the Violent Crime Control and Law Enforcement Act of 1994. The crime bill contained another rules change of potential benefit to plaintiffs in sexual harassment cases. Sponsored by Republican Senator Bob Dole and Republican Congresswoman Susan Molinari (R-New York) and endorsed by the Clinton Justice Department, evidence rules 413, 414, and 415 made evidence of prior sexual assault by a defendant — whether proven or merely alleged — admissible in federal sexual assault and child molestation cases. Rules 413 and 414 govern federal criminal actions against sexual offenders; rule 415 liberalized evidence gathering in federal civil actions against them. According to the rule, an assault target seeking civil sanctions such as compensatory or punitive damages can explore evidence that her assailant has done it before to

92. "President Clinton's Opposition to Plaintiff's Motion to Reconsider the Court's December 18, 1997 Order," *Jones v. Clinton*, Civil Action No. LR-C-94-290, January 7, 1998.

strengthen her credibility before juries or even to corroborate her claim. Rule 415 applies only to claims for federal remedies, which are available principally when sex offenses and discrimination intersect. Hence, the rule will be most relevant to plaintiffs seeking damages under Title VII, Section 1983, or the Violence Against Women Act.

The rule covers all acts the U.S. Code defines as criminal sexual assault. It reaches physical sexual harassment in the workplace — unwanted or unilateral sexualized touching — including the physical contact Paula Jones alleged President Clinton imposed on her.[93] It entitled Paula Jones to collect discovery testimony from Kathleen Willey, for example, who reported that President Clinton groped her and pulled her hand to his groin. According to Jones's lawyers and Judge Susan Webber Wright, it also permitted Jones to inquire into Monica Lewinsky's rumored physical relationship with the president to determine whether, if the relationship did exist, it was based on coercion and fear.[94]

The new rules have met with strong criticism from jurists and civil libertarians who read them as mandating highly prejudicial "propensity" evidence that undermines a defendant's rights. At least in the sexual harassment context, however, the few courts that have heard Rule 415 cases have subjected challenged evidence to close review for probativeness and prejudice.[95] Applied this way, Rule 415 establishes a new rebuttable presumption, not a new absolute requirement. Although this interpretation mitigates some of the effects of Rule 415, it leaves intact an imbalance between plaintiffs' and defendants' vulnerability to character evidence in sex cases. Rule 415 reverses for defendants the presumptions Rule 412 establishes for plaintiffs. Defendants' prior similar acts are admissible unless the court is persuaded that the evidence is too prejudicial; plaintiffs'

93. Charles Alan Wright and Kenneth W. Graham, Jr., *Federal Practice and Procedure: Federal Rules of Evidence, 1998 Supplement* (1998) Chapter 5, Section 5412B; *Jones v. Clinton*, 993 F. Supp. 1217 (E.D. Arkansas, 1998).

94. "Plaintiff's Memorandum in Opposition to the Motion of Defendant Clinton to Limit Discovery," *Jones v. Clinton*, Civil Action No. LR-C-94-290, November 3, 1997; *Jones v. Clinton*, 993 F. Supp. 1217.

95. *Frank v. County of Hudson*, 924 F. Supp. 620 (D. New Jersey, 1996); *Cleveland v. KFC National Management Company*, 948 F. Supp. 62 (N.D. Georgia, Atlanta Division, 1996).

prior conduct, on the other hand, is inadmissible unless the court is persuaded that it is more probative than prejudicial.[96]

Rules 413–415 are likely to attract controversy for some time to come, as courts struggle to bring them under the due process protections of other evidence rules.[97] Although Rule 415 might strengthen the legal position of some targets of physical sexual harassment, the rule actually is not necessary for plaintiffs to introduce "pattern and practice" evidence. As the first court to hear a Rule 415 case in the sexual harassment context pointed out, "even before the effective date of the new evidence rules, courts have allowed such evidence to counteract the problem that arises frequently in sexual cases when an absence of witnesses reduces the case to a 'swearing contest' between the defendant and the alleged victim."[98] In both race and sex cases — and in both physical and verbal harassment cases — courts generally have followed evidence rules 401, 403, and 404(b) to consider information about the defendant's conduct toward other employees. They also have followed Federal Rule of Civil Procedure 26(b) to permit wide-ranging pretrial discovery of any information that "appears reasonably calculated to lead to . . . admissible evidence."[99] Courts variously have argued that "any sexual harassment by [the defendant] is relevant . . . whether of plaintiff or of others,"[100] because it might rebut a defendant's claim that a harassed employee was fired for cause; might prove that a work environment is hostile; might establish an employer's liability; or might show that the alleged conduct probably occurred.[101]

96. Jane Harris Aiken, "Sexual Character Evidence in Civil Actions: Refining the Propensity Rule," *Wisconsin Law Review* 1997 (1997): 1221–1272; Michael S. Ellis, "The Politics Behind Federal Rules of Evidence 413, 414, and 415," *Santa Clara Law Review* 38 (1998): 961–988; Daniel L. Overbey, "Federal Rule of Evidence 415 and *Paula Corbin Jones v. William Jefferson Clinton:* The Use of Propensity Evidence in Sexual Harassment Suits," *Notre Dame Journal of Law, Ethics and Public Policy* 12 (1998): 343–368.

97. John Gibeaut, "An Evidentiary Dragnet: Courts Remain Wary in Introducing Uncharged Sex Crimes," *ABA Journal* 84 (June 1998): 44.

98. *Frank v. County of Hudson,* at 626.

99. *Stalnaker v. Kmart Corporation,* 1996 WL 397563 (D. Kansas, 1996). 100. Ibid., at 4.

101. *Phillips v. Smalley Maintenance Services, Inc.,* 711 F. 2d. 1524 (11th Cir., 1983); *Hunter v. Allis-Chalmers Corp.,* 797 F. 2d. 1417 (7th Cir., 1986);

The admissibility of probative evidence of an alleged harasser's unwelcome sexual conduct toward other women in the workplace has aided plaintiffs in establishing credibility in what often is a lopsided legal contest. Conservative Judge Richard Posner explained why other similar acts of workplace discrimination need to be considered: "Given the difficulty of proving employment discrimination — the employer will deny it, and almost every worker has some deficiency on which the employer can plausibly blame the worker's troubles — a flat rule that evidence of other discriminatory acts by or attributable to the employer can never be admitted . . . would be unjustified."[102]

Sexual harassment targets are structurally disadvantaged by their position on the employment hierarchy when they challenge their harassers, particularly if they are lone complainants without witnesses to corroborate their stories. They are also politically disadvantaged by a myriad of social attitudes: that good women don't get harassed, that well-adjusted women don't let it bother them, and that nice women don't complain about it. Women's structural and political disadvantages intercept justice by placing women, not their harassers, under suspicion. One judge recently justified this suspicion by paraphrasing the old adage about rape: "A charge of sexual harassment is easy to make and difficult to defend."[103]

The new Rule 412 attenuates some of the political liabilities sexual harassment plaintiffs bring into the legal process. We can hope that combined with the admission of "pattern" evidence, the new rule will improve women's opportunities to win vindication in court. Yet each woman's vindication should not depend on another woman being harassed. Until the word of just one woman counts, potential plaintiffs will be deterred by the suffocating doubt with which each woman's harassment story is received.

Albright v. Longview Police Department, 884 F. 2d. 835 (5th Cir., 1989); *Robinson v. Jacksonville Shipyards, Inc.,* 760 F. Supp. 1486 (M.D. Florida, 1991); *Webb v. Hyman,* 861 F. Supp. 1094 (D. D.C., 1994).

102. Quoted in *Webb v. Hyman,* at 1111.

103. *Shea v. Galaxie Lumber & Construction Company, Ltd.,* 1996 WL 111890 (N.D. Illinois, 1996), at 1.

First introduced in 1990 by then-Representative Barbara Boxer (D-California) and Senator Joseph Biden, the 1994 Violence Against Women Act marked a triumph for feminism. Enacted by the Congress that had been elected in the Year of the Woman, the act authorized funding to improve safety for women in public transit and public parks, to promote rape prevention education, to establish a national domestic violence hotline, to set up battered women's shelters, to conduct a study on campus sexual assault, and to train judges and police officers about sex crimes and domestic violence. In these ways, VAWA expressly recognized how private violence vitiates women's public rights. But VAWA did more than assign public resources to fix women's private troubles. It also punctured the seal of privacy that for so long has protected some of men's most dangerous prerogatives in their personal relations with women. It did this most strikingly when it created a new substantive right to be free of gender-motivated violence and backed up the right with monetary and injunctive remedies.[104]

The civil rights remedy for gender violence culminated feminist efforts to expose the nexus between sexualized and domestic violence and women's inequality. It also culminated feminist efforts to put recovery from violence into women's own hands by establishing a cause for civil action. Congressional committee reports documented the failures of state criminal justice systems in handling crimes against women, demonstrating how states discriminate against women when they refuse to prosecute rape or battery — for example — just because a husband or a date did it.[105] The reports also illuminated the public effects of women's private injuries, effects that toll both the

104. H.R. 3355 (P.L. 103-322) Subtitle C, "Civil Rights for Women," Section 40302 (b) [Right to be Free from Crimes of Violence] and (c) [Cause of Action].

105. U. S. Senate, *Report No. 103-138*, Violence Against Women Act of 1993 (Washington, D.C., 1993); U.S. House of Representatives, *Report No. 103-95*, Violence Against Women Act of 1993 (Washington, D.C., 1993), 26; U.S. Senate, *Report No. 102-197*, Violence Against Women Act (Washington, D.C., 1991), 44–48; United States Senate, *Report No. 101-545*, Violence Against Women Act (Washington, D.C., 1990), 33.

economy and women's opportunities.[106] The VAWA civil rights remedy gives women an alternative to the criminal justice system: they may seek civil judgments against their abusers even when states will not pursue criminal convictions. In addition, VAWA's civil rights remedy gives targets of violent sexual harassment an alternative to the limited awards available under Title VII. Finally, the civil rights remedy invites women to advance equality by avenging the violence that locks us to our gender roles and positions. Practically speaking, most perpetrators outside the employment context will not be able to afford the monetary relief women may win for their injuries. Still, at the very least, the VAWA remedy enables women to win physical relief from further injury and thereby vindicate our right to be free of sexual and gender violence.[107]

The future of the VAWA remedy is uncertain, however, for its constitutionality has been challenged. Nevertheless, it is a benchmark in the long struggle of powerless people to secure equality by claiming and confirming their rights as individuals. As with Sections 1981 and 1983, and as with Title VII, the VAWA remedy attacks inequality by making certain acts that enforce inequality causes for civil action. Unlike criminal proceedings, civil actions do not depend on government initiative, on government's attitude toward individuals who allege injury, or on government's determination that a harm to one person constitutes an offense against society. Civil actions belong to individuals. When we bring a civil action, we usually seek restitution for a wrong perpetrated by private institutions or by other individuals. In the civil rights context, we bring civil actions not only to recover for personal harm but also to enforce government's prohibition on discrimination. Hence, far from being "*only a*

106. U.S. House of Representatives, *Report No. 103-711*, Violent Crime Control in Law Enforcement Act of 1994 (Washington, D.C., 1994), 385; S. *Report 103-138*, 54.

107. Victoria F. Nourse, "Where Violence, Relationship, and Equality Meet: The Violence Against Women Act's Civil Rights Remedy," *Wisconsin Women's Law Journal* 11 (Summer 1996): 1–36; Lisa Barre-Quick and Shannon Matthew Kasley, "The Road Less Traveled: Obstacles in the Path of the Effective Use of the Civil Rights Provision of the Violence Against Women Act in the Employment Context," *Seton Hall Constitutional Law Journal* 8 (Spring 1998): 415–457.

civil case," as President Clinton's defenders would have it, a sexual harassment lawsuit advances the democratically decided goal of gender equality in employment (and education) by securing the rights of individual women.

The civil actions authorized by civil rights law may belong to us as individuals, but when we pursue a civil rights action we do so for the collective ends of equality and justice. For this reason, civil rights actions are weighty with public purpose. Yet they also are inherently fragile. Legislated by Congress, our employment, education, and gender violence rights depend on favorable political majorities. We know from experience that when the bearers of rights are unpopular, their rights are unpopular, too. Only a few short years ago, the most demonized women in America — mothers who need welfare — lost basic rights.[108] If the ritual trashing of high-profile sexual harassment targets is any indication, sexually harassed women are unpopular as well. Indeed, the politics surrounding *Jones v. Clinton* suggests that not even feminists believe that every woman's word should count or that the law should promote the justice interests of every woman who needs it. Will the rights of sexual harassment targets be the next to go?

108. Gwendolyn Mink, *Welfare's End* (Cornell University Press, 1998).

f o u r **Bill Clinton's Regime of Disbelief**

n June 1998, the Supreme Court handed down two decisions
that improved sexually harassed women's access to civil rights
remedies. Before these two decisions, a target who had been
harassed but not punished by her supervisor could not win relief under Title VII unless she could prove that her employer "knew
or should have known" about the harassment.[1] In *Faragher v. City of
Boca Raton* and in *Burlington Industries v. Ellerth*, the Court decided
that employers are vicariously liable whenever employees are sexu-

---

1. Some courts have held supervisors individually liable under agency
principles. Elizabeth R. Koller Whittenbury, "Individual Liability for
Sexual Harassment Under Federal Law," *The Labor Lawyer* 14 (Fall 1998):
357–373.

ally harassed by supervisors.[2] This means, among other things, that a target does not have to prove she suffered economic harm to recover damages from her employer if she was harassed by someone with formal power over her. Nor does she have to prove that her employer knew about the harassment. An employer may escape liability under the decisions, but only if it can establish that it tried to prevent and correct the harassment and that the target "unreasonably" failed to take advantage of its preventive or corrective policies "or to otherwise avoid harm."[3] Reasoning that "there is a sense in which a harassing supervisor *is always assisted in his misconduct by the supervisory relationship*,"[4] the Court recognized that sexual harassment involving supervisors is never "just about sex" but always implicates employment decisions, even if only implicitly. Hence, the Court concluded, where there is an unequal employment relationship, a target's right to relief flows from her harasser's power over her.[5]

The new rules for employer liability will be a real help to women who can convince judges and juries that their supervisors really did sexually harass them. When, whether, and which women will be convincing remains an open question, however, for while the Court improved access to remedies in 1998, it did not improve women's prospects for being believed. More important, even as the Court opened access to remedies at law, the politics of sexual harassment clamped down on women who seek to use the law. A political collision between erstwhile proponents of sexual harassment law and Paula Jones's sexual harassment case helped to consolidate the regime of disbelief.

Paula Jones filed suit against President Bill Clinton in May 1994, alleging that, in 1991, while he was governor of Arkansas, Clinton had invited her up to his hotel room, where he touched her inappropriately, exposed his penis, asked her to kiss it, fondled it when she would not, implicitly threatened her, and reminded her of his power

---

2. *Faragher v. City of Boca Raton*, 1998 WL 336322 (U.S.) [524 U.S. 775 (1998)]; *Burlington Industries v. Ellerth*, 1998 WL 336326 (U.S.) [524 U.S. 742. (1998) 876].

3. *Burlington Industries v. Ellerth*, at 15.

4. My italics.

5. *Faragher v. City of Boca Raton*, at 17.

over her.[6] Jones's original complaint charged Clinton with several related offenses: infringing her Fourteenth Amendment rights, conspiring to do so, intentionally inflicting emotional distress, and defamation.[7] Because the statute of limitations for Jones's right to relief under Title VII had expired by the time she brought her suit, she stated her claim under Sections 1983 and 1985 of federal civil rights law, as well as under the Arkansas law of outrage. The gravamen of her complaint was that Clinton had sexually harassed her, subjecting her both "to the fear of losing [her] job or of having to provide sex to the Governor as a quid pro quo for keeping her job" and "to fear of losing . . . a proper and pleasant work environment."[8]

Clinton filed a motion to dismiss the case, arguing that he was immune from civil litigation so long as he was president. In a unanimous opinion, the Supreme Court rejected Clinton's claim in May 1997, permitting Jones to proceed with her case.[9] At that point, district court judge Susan Webber Wright began to manage the discovery process, the phase of evidence-gathering that precedes a trial. As do many sexual harassment plaintiffs, Jones sought to enhance her credibility or perhaps even to substantiate her allegation with "pattern and practice" evidence showing that Clinton had engaged in sexually harassing behavior before. The judge granted Jones's request to depose Clinton and certain "other women" about his sexual conduct toward women subordinates in the workplace, including toward women who may have submitted to his sexual requests.[10]

Monica Lewinsky, a former White House intern and employee, was one of the women Jones subpoenaed to depose on this score. On January 21, 1998, we learned that Lewinsky might have had a sexual relationship with the president, that she might have filed a false

6. "Complaint," *Jones v. Clinton*, May 1994.

7. Ibid., paragraphs 58–79.

8. Ibid., paragraph 62.

9. *Clinton v. Jones*, 520 U.S. 681 (1997).

10. E.g., "Order," *Jones v. Clinton*, No. LR-C-94-290, December 11, 1997. The judge also permitted Jones to discover information "regarding any individuals . . . whose liaisons with Governor Clinton were procured, protected, concealed, and/or facilitated by State Troopers assigned to the governor."

affidavit about it in response to Jones's queries, and that the president might have encouraged her to do so.[11] The president's flat-out televised denial of any kind of sexual relationship with "that woman" raised the possibility that he might have lied in his own sworn deposition in the Jones case.[12] Soon we learned that the president might have orchestrated a cover-up of truthful evidence to which Jones was entitled.

Following the Lewinsky revelations, the president, his wife, and their political friends launched a campaign to discredit allegations of presidential perjury and obstruction of justice in the Jones case. The president spun malicious gossip that Lewinsky was troubled, a vamp, and a "stalker."[13] Hillary Clinton denounced the allegations as the concoction of "a vast right-wing conspiracy."[14] Their friends took these messages to the airwaves. In a yearlong barrage of sound bites, Clinton's friends chorused that if the president had lied, he had done so in "only a civil case" and that the lies had been "just about sex." When, in his August 17, 1998 confession of an "inappropriate" re-

11. Susan Schmidt, Peter Baker, and Toni Locy, "Clinton Accused of Urging Aide to Lie," *Washington Post*, January 21, 1998. The *Post* was the first to run the story.

12. On the day the story broke, Clinton told PBS in a televised interview that "there is not a sexual relationship, an improper relationship, or any other improper relationship." On January 26, 1998, he told reporters after a White House news event that "I did not have sexual relations with that woman. . . . I never told anybody to lie." http://www.cnn.com/US/9801/21/clinton.starr.pm/index.html, Wolf Blitzer, "Clinton Denies Affair with Intern, Coverup," CNN, January 21, 1998; Associated Press, "Key Events in Starr Investigation," September 11, 1998.

13. See, e.g., testimony of former White House aide Sidney Blumenthal indicating that the day the Lewinsky story became public (January 21, 1998) the president told him that Lewinsky was known as "the stalker," had come on to him, and had threatened to tell people that they had an affair even though they did not. Blumenthal so testified before a grand jury in June 1998 and in a videotaped deposition during the president's impeachment trial on February 3, 1999. The latter was aired by House managers during their closing argument on February 6, 1999.

14. Hillary Clinton made this much-publicized statement on the *Today Show* on January 27, 1998.

lationship with Monica Lewinsky, Clinton declared that his sex lies are "nobody's business,"[15] his friends leapt to defend his privacy and damned Paula Jones's right to truthful evidence as "sexual McCarthyism."[16]

Among the president's defenders were leading feminists. Abandoning the procedural rigors feminists long had fought for in sexual harassment cases, they lent a feminist imprimatur to a sexual harassment defendant's disrespect for the law. With few notable exceptions, feminists excused the president's lies by pooh-poohing the Jones case — as if the weaker the case, the more acceptable it is to dissemble evidence in it. Some well-placed feminists also disparaged women whose testimony might have established a pattern of sexually harassing behavior by Clinton — as if the more imperfect the woman, the less significant her possible harassment. Leading feminists further shielded defendant Clinton's sexual conduct toward employees behind the walls of privacy and consent — as if the more intrusive the behavior, the less easily should a woman challenge it.

In these ways, many feminists entered the regime of disbelief, where they divided the world into women whose rights should be defended and those whose rights need not. This double standard not only expels some women from the sisterhood feminism is supposed to promote but also protects some men — like the president — from women who stand up for themselves and claim their rights.

Feminism did not require us to "believe Anita Hill" in the literal sense, but it did require us to insist that everyone take seriously what she had to say. It requires us to give any sexually harassed woman the presumption of truthfulness just as we give her defendant the presumption of innocence. Likewise, feminism did not compel us literally to believe Paula Jones, but it did compel us to insist that every sexually harassed woman gets to have her say in a scrupulously fair le-

15. President Bill Clinton, Address to the Nation, August 17, 1998. http://www.cnn.com/ALLPOLITICS/1998/08/17/speech, "Clinton Admits to 'Wrong' Relationship with Lewinsky."

16. I don't know who first used this phrase during the Clinton inquiry and impeachment. Alan Dershowitz published a book with the phrase as its title during the impeachment controversy. *Sexual McCarthyism: Clinton, Starr, and the Emerging Constitutional Crisis* (New York, 1998).

gal proceeding, even if we don't like her friends and even if we like the defendant. Yet, inside the regime of disbelief many feminists short-circuited Paula Jones's legal process. Substituting public impressions for jury deliberations, they arrogated to themselves the prescience to judge the merits of Jones's case and joined presidential efforts to supplant issues of fact with questions of motive.[17] Not only did feminists preempt the legal process by judging Paula Jones, they also disdained her right to evidence that might have helped her win a different legal — and public — judgment. One of the ways many feminists — and other Clinton defenders — disdained Jones's right to evidence was by disdaining the evidence itself. In this they helped Bill Clinton change the national subject from lies about evidence in a sexual harassment case to lies about an intimate relationship. Transposing a woman's right to public remedies into a man's right to privacy, leading feminists beat a retreat from a law they helped forge, and in some respects they beat a retreat from feminism itself.

JUDGING PAULA JONES

Judge Wright dismissed Paula Jones's case on April 1, 1998. Wright rejected Jones's claim of quid pro quo harassment for lack of a "tangible job detriment." She also rejected Jones's claim of hostile environment harassment for the same reason. Departing from the Supreme Court's precedent in *Meritor*,[18] the judge noted that a lack of evidence of "adverse employment actions" resulting in "materially significant disadvantage . . . dispel the notion that [Jones] was subjected to a hostile work environment."[19] She further departed from Supreme Court precedent — *Harris v. Forklift Systems*[20] — to suggest that without proof of tangible psychological injury, Jones could not show that she had suffered a hostile work environment. Finally, she maintained that for a single incident to count as sexual harassment, it must have been "exceptional . . . such as an assault," not merely

17. Jeffrey Toobin quotes Senator Daniel Patrick Moynihan to make a similar point in "Pat 'N Bill," *The New Yorker* (February 8, 1999), 30.
18. *Meritor Savings Bank v. Vinson*, 477 U.S. 57 (1986).
19. *Jones v. Clinton*, 1998 WL 148370 (E.D. Arkansas) at 14.
20. *Harris v. Forklift Systems, Inc.*, 510 U.S. 17 (1993).

"boorish and offensive" as had been Clinton's alleged behavior toward Jones.[21] The judge grossly distorted the hostile environment framework in these ways, foreclosing legal remedies for Paula Jones and potentially for future hostile environment plaintiffs (at least in Arkansas) as well.

National Organization for Women president Patricia Ireland roundly condemned the judge's suggestion that a single unwelcome physical advance doesn't count as harassment unless the perpetrator physically brutalizes his target.[22] Yet, three weeks later, at a news conference celebrating oral argument in the Ellerth case, Ireland insisted that it was Jones's appeal, not Judge Wright's ruling, that "would injure everyday women in the workplace."[23] Hence, Ireland explained, NOW would not contribute a friend-of-the-court brief to support Jones's appeal. Drawing conclusions about Jones's evidence even though Jones had not had a chance to present it at trial, Ireland determined that Jones's was an "imperfect case." Ireland supported her conclusion by citing Judge Wright's finding that Jones had not suffered tangible consequences as a result of Clinton's alleged harassment. She further denounced Jones's "disreputable right-wing" friends, asserting that to defend Jones would be to advance their cause.[24]

Ireland was not the only feminist to deprecate Jones's alleged harassment. Throughout the yearlong investigation, then impeachment, of Bill Clinton for perjury and obstruction of justice in the Jones case, many leading feminists disputed that Jones had been sexually harassed *even if what she said happened in the Little Rock hotel room was true*. To be sure, some feminists, such as Martha Davis of the NOW-Legal Defense and Education Fund and trailblazing

21. *Jones v. Clinton*, 1998 WL148370, at 15, 17.

22. "Statement of NOW President Patricia Ireland on Dismissal of Jones Case; Ruling Does Not Mean Open Season on Women in the Workforce," press release, April 2, 1998.

23. "Statement of NOW President Patricia Ireland on *Burlington Industries v. Ellerth*; NOW's Initiative to Stop Sexual Harassment," press release, April 22, 1998.

24. Ibid.; "Patricia Ireland Holds News Conference on the *Ellerth v. Burlington Industries* Sexual Harassment Case," *Washington Transcript Service*, April 22, 1998.

legal scholar Catharine MacKinnon, expressed divergent views.[25] But in the main, such opinion leaders as Gloria Steinem, Irene Natividad, Anita Hill, Eleanor Smeal, Betty Friedan, and Susan Estrich found one reason or another to expel Jones's alleged experience from the rubric of sexual harassment — or to exonerate the president altogether.

Gloria Steinem described the Jones case as "borderline . . . at best, because it had no job — no demonstrable job consequences. It didn't take place in the workplace."[26] Irene Natividad, former head of the National Women's Political Caucus, agreed, saying that Judge Wright's "decision expressed the discomfort a lot of us had. . . . There has to be a kind of retribution and that never appeared."[27] Anita Hill opined on *Meet the Press* that the Jones case was "missing . . . the discrimination element . . . I have a hard time finding any adverse ramifications for her in terms of her employment."[28] Eleanor Smeal, president of the Feminist Majority, echoed, asserting that Jones had failed to prove that she had suffered. "Plus," Smeal explained, "when she said 'No,' it stopped. . . . Most women d[on't] think it was a big deal. A lot of people would say, 'Boy, you ought to see what's happened to me.'"[29] Betty Friedan repeated the thought: "If she says 'no' and he walks away, what's the big deal?"[30] Feminist legal scholar and commentator Susan Estrich took these doubts and pejoratives one step further, arguing that Clinton "has more class" than to be a

25. Martha Davis, legal director of the NOW-Legal Defense and Education Fund (an entity separate from NOW), explained the problem with Judge Wright's ruling thusly: "You look at the totality of the circumstances, and we don't believe the judge did that here. She didn't discuss the impact of the power differential and the way it would impact the context of his behavior." Quoted in Harvey Berkman and Marcia Coyle, "And If Jones Does Appeal?" *The National Law Journal* (April 13, 1998).

26. Gloria Steinem, interview, "Women React to Jones Dismissal," *Morning Edition*, NPR, April 2, 1998.

27. Thomas B. Edsall and Terry M. Neal, "Response to Dismissal Has Partisan Flavor," *Washington Post*, April 2, 1998.

28. Anita Hill, interview, *Meet the Press*, NBC, March 22, 1998.

29. http://allpolitics.com/1998/04/07/ap/feminist/index.html, Michelle Boorstein, "Feminists Split on Jones Ruling."

30. Ann Gerhart and Annie Groer, "The Reliable Source: Friedan on Jones," *Washington Post*, April 23, 1998.

harasser: "Rapists and harassers are not generally sexy guys who like women and step over the line."[31]

It seems that to most of these feminists, what Jones said happened to her didn't really count as harassment because Clinton didn't follow up the incident either with a tangibly adverse employment action or with further sexual abuse. None of these feminists even considered (publicly, at least) the subjective effects of sexual harassment where power differentials are extreme, as between a governor and a secretary — effects that make harassment discrimination *in itself,* not only in its aftermath. Stunningly absent from most feminist commentary on the Jones case was any concern for how a subordinate might feel about herself and her work when her superior asks her to service him sexually. This led one civil rights attorney to comment: "Anyone who doesn't believe that taking down of someone's pants who's an employer in front of an employee does not constitute a hostile work environment is kind of off touch with reality."[32]

When many feminists joined legions of Democrats to contest the merits of Jones's claim, they may have been out of touch with sexual harassment law. Whatever their level of legal understanding, their legal discourse compromised the law by raising the threshold for harassment virtually to require either a quid pro quo or sexual assault in all cases where the perpetrator does not repeat his conduct with the same woman. That feminists weighed in with such a restrictive approach to sexual harassment is especially disturbing because the status of single incidents in sexual harassment law has not yet been settled. In fact, the Supreme Court in *Ellerth* expressly reserved judgment "as to whether a single unfulfilled threat is sufficient to constitute discrimination in the terms or conditions of employment."[33]

Not only did many feminists define harassment in terms of its tangible harms, some among them defined it in terms of its frequency or repetition. For example, in apparent agreement with Judge Wright's argument that though "odious," what Bill Clinton did to

31. Katherine Q. Seelye, "'He Said, She Said' and They Clammed Up," *New York Times,* January 18, 1997.

32. Linda Kenney, interview, "Women React to Jones Dismissal," *Morning Edition,* NPR, April 2, 1998.

33. *Burlington Industries v. Ellerth,* at 8.

Paula Jones (if true) was still only "a mere proposition,"[34] Gloria Steinem wrote in *Ms.* that "gross as the alleged proposal was, Clinton took no for an answer . . . [it was] a one-time unwelcome event outside the workplace."[35] Distinguishing between Bill Clinton, on the one hand, and former Senator Bob Packwood and Justice Clarence Thomas, on the other, she went on to explain that Packwood had harassed many women multiple times while Thomas had harassed one woman many times. According to Steinem's logic, since "mutual consent . . . [is] the bedrock of sexual harassment law," a harasser gets to hit on each woman once to see if she will consent.[36] Feminist writer Susan Faludi concurred with this line of reasoning in a piece published in the *Guardian Weekly.*[37] So did Betty Friedan. In an April 1998 comment on the Jones-Lewinsky-Willey allegations, she asked what's the big deal if he took no for an answer?[38] In a September 1998 interview with CNN, she elaborated, saying that former White House volunteer Kathleen Willey "should have slapped his [the president's] face for christ's sake" when he groped her and that a woman who doesn't want a man's hand on her breast should just take it off. Again, "what's the big deal? It's not that big a deal."[39]

Women have been struggling for years to make the law responsive, not only to harassment when it is objectively extreme, but also to harassment because it subjectively subordinates. Feminists who defended President Clinton because he didn't force Jones to give him oral sex, didn't ask her for it more than once, and didn't fire her when she refused him undermined this struggle. By throwing in with the view that sexual harassment must be multiple and egregious to be a legally cognizable problem, feminists popularized it. They thereby normalized serial sexual harassment.

34. *Jones v. Clinton*, 1998 WL 148370, at 17.

35. Gloria Steinem, "Yes Means Yes, No Means No: Why Sex Scandals Don't Mean Harassment," *Ms.* (May/June 1998), 63.

36. Ibid., 62.

37. Susan Faludi, "Damned If You Don't, Damned If You Do," *Guardian Weekly*, August 30, 1998.

38. Gerhart and Groer, "Friedan on Jones."

39. Betty Friedan, interview, *Newstand: Time*, CNN, date uncertain (ca. September 20, 1998). Author's videotape file.

Women also have been struggling for some time to enhance their credibility in sexual harassment proceedings. One way to improve women's credibility is through the use of "pattern and practice" evidence of a defendant's similar acts, which can be especially useful in counterbalancing the credibility a defendant enjoys by virtue of his formal power or social station. Feminists undermined women's advances in the legal process by trivializing the Monica Lewinsky "pattern" evidence to which the law said Jones was entitled. As we shall see, one way many feminists trivialized the Lewinsky evidence was by dubbing it "just about sex." Another way was by insisting that the evidence was immaterial.

Jones had sought information from Lewinsky as part of the discovery process, a process that ordinarily can be sheathed in protective orders guarding confidentiality under evidence rule 412, which covers "pattern" witnesses as well as plaintiffs. With the discovery of the Lewinsky story by third parties, including the press, however, the process spun out of control. Then, at the request of the Independent Counsel, Judge Wright decided to exclude the Lewinsky evidence from the Jones trial because of the concurrent criminal investigation into possible presidential perjury and obstruction of justice. The Judge wrote of the Lewinsky evidence, "it simply is not essential to the core issues in this case" and noted that "[Jones] does not argue that her case depends solely on the Lewinsky evidence." Moreover, the Judge maintained, Jones would have to await the outcome of the criminal investigation to use the Lewinsky evidence, which would drag out the resolution of her case.[40]

Many feminists, with other Clinton defenders, twisted the Judge's characterization of the Lewinsky evidence as "not essential" into a finding that the evidence was *immaterial* to Jones's case. This fueled arguments that alleged presidential lies about Monica Lewinsky were unimportant — because the subject of the lies (Lewinsky) was irrelevant to the proceeding (*Jones v. Clinton*) in which the lies were told. Shortly before the President's grand jury testimony aired publicly in September 1998, Patricia Ireland underscored the point: "no good prosecutor . . . would bring a perjury charge based on a deposition in

40. "Memorandum and Order," *Jones v. Clinton*, No. LR-C-94-290, March 9, 1998, at 4.

a lawsuit where that deposition was ruled immaterial."[41] In other words, a defendant is free to lie about evidence if his lies help rule out consideration of the evidence.

In the course of belittling Jones's claim, many feminists either betrayed their ignorance of a law they have heretofore championed or belied their commitment to equal justice. Defining sexual harassment in terms of consequences rather than actions — in terms of the paychecks and doctor bills of the target rather than the unwelcome conduct of the perpetrator — they eschewed the hostile environment framework established in *Meritor* and *Harris*. Defining sexual harassment in terms of repetition rather than impact, they gave a free pass to serial harassers. Ignoring the power dynamics behind sexual harassment, meanwhile, they also shunned the premise of employer liability established in *Faragher* and *Ellerth*.

Feminists who scoffed at Jones's harassment claim because they could not see tangible injuries sent a message to women that unless they fit into the quid pro quo framework, their harassment probably isn't the real thing. Those who scoffed at Jones's harassment claim because Clinton did it to her only once sent a message to women that the first time their employers grope them is no big deal: every boss gets one free hit. Those who scoffed at the pattern evidence Jones sought entrenched women's structural disadvantage against defendants who steal credibility from their position. These feminist turns added to the fragility of sexual harassment law, opening it to renewed political scrutiny and ridicule and thereby threatening its legal future.

DISSING "OTHER WOMEN"

A number of feminist leaders diminished the pattern evidence Jones sought either by disputing its relevance to sexual harassment or by disparaging the women involved. Take Kathleen Willey, who told *Sixty Minutes* that while she was a White House volunteer, President Clinton had groped her breast and put her hand on his genitals.[42] Many feminist notables actually were shaken by her story. Patricia Ireland spoke out about Willey's "very serious allegation" in numer-

41. Patricia Ireland, interview, *Sunday Today*, NBC, date uncertain (ca. September 20, 1998). Author's videotape file.

42. Kathleen Willey, interview, *Sixty Minutes*, CBS, March 15, 1998.

ous television interviews, saying that "if her story is true, it is not just sexual harassment, it's sexual assault."[43] Kate Michelman, president of the National Abortion Rights Action League, said in an interview, "it's alarming. [Mrs. Willey] . . . sounded credible and it's a new problem for the president."[44]

But other feminists rejected Willey's allegations as somewhat frivolous and quite beyond the scope of sexual harassment law. Gloria Steinem, for example, wrote in the *New York Times* that the "basis of sexual harassment law" is "no means no; yes means yes." Hence, she argued, even if Willey's allegations were true, the president would not be guilty of sexual harassment: "He is accused of having made a gross, dumb and reckless pass at a supporter during a low point in her life. She pushed him away . . . and it never happened again. In other words, President Clinton took 'no' for an answer." In a surprisingly hostile assessment, Steinem also wrote that Willey was "old enough to be Monica Lewinsky's mother," as if Willey's age somehow discredited her story. Moreover, Steinem followed the Clinton pattern of twisting troubling facts into questions of their tellers' motives. Suggesting that Willey's "dead husband's debts" might have something to do with the story she told, Steinem damned Willey with feigned understanding: "If any of the other women had tried to sell their stories to a celebrity tell-all book publisher, as Ms. Willey did, you might be even more skeptical about their motives. But with her, you think, 'Well, she needs the money.'"[45]

Similarly, White House feminist Ann Lewis sowed doubt about Willey, disclosing on the *Today Show* the morning after the Willey interview "a personal experience of my own which confirms the president's [denial]." Saying she only wanted to be "informative, never accusatory,"[46] Lewis recounted how Willey had come to her in

43. "Statement of NOW President Patricia Ireland on Kathleen Willey's Testimony," press release, March 16, 1998.

44. Richard L. Berke, "Willey Interview Shakes Clinton's Support among Women," *New York Times*, March 17, 1998.

45. Gloria Steinem, "Feminists and the Clinton Question," *New York Times*, March 22, 1998.

46. Richard L. Berke, "Women's Groups in a Bind Over Willey," *New York Times*, March 18, 1998.

1996 — two and a half years after the president had groped her — to say that she wanted to work on Clinton's reelection campaign: "She made a point of telling me . . . very positively how much she admired the president. . . . So I couldn't tell you how surprised I was to see her last night, because there was such a contradiction between what I saw and heard last night and the person I met with in 1996."[47] Lewis's professed "surprise" was part of a White House strategy of disbelief. The strategy included releasing friendly letters Willey had written to the president after the incident and otherwise portraying her as a liar who was just in it for the money.

Other well-placed feminists responded skeptically to the Willey story, reminding the public that the president deserved the benefit of the doubt. Then-Senator Carol Moseley Braun told a news conference that "inasmuch as there is a process at work, I think we have a responsibility to take him at his word."[48] Senator Barbara Boxer, who had demanded Senator Bob Packwood's resignation when he faced accusations of sexual harassment, likewise observed, "Mrs. Willey has made serious charges and they deserve to be thoroughly investigated. . . . It should also be noted that the President has unequivocally denied these charges."[49] Feminist icon and Clinton defender Geraldine Ferraro, once a Democratic vice-presidential nominee, revealed her contempt for Willey's story when she refused even to hear it: "I haven't gotten the tape of Paula Jones, so why would I get the tape of this? I can't assess what's real and what's not real. And I don't want to."[50]

Monica Lewinsky aroused even less sympathy among feminists than did Kathleen Willey. During the long months of presidential prevarication, prominent feminists depicted 24-year-old Lewinsky as a predator and the president as her victim — leaving utterly unexamined the power relationship between the two. Feminists did not invent this topsy-turvy narrative; Bill Clinton did. But many repeated it and based their commentary on it, setting feminism to the

47. Ann Lewis, interview, *Today Show*, NBC, March 16, 1998.
48. Terry M. Neal and Ceci Connolly, "Scandal Snags Three Female Incumbents," *Washington Post*, March 28, 1998.
49. Berke, "Willey Interview Shakes Clinton's Support among Women."
50. Ibid.

task of trashing women. As one congresswoman told the *New York Times* only days after the Lewinsky story broke: "We are not falling on our swords for these types of women, Paula Jones or Gennifer Flowers. . . . We do not see Monica as some little naif here."[51] Even Barbara Ehrenreich, in an essay that took principal aim at feminists, dabbled in some Monica-bashing: "if Monica was a kind of harasser herself . . . feminists [still] have plenty of reasons to be incensed about the gender dynamics of the Clinton White House. We're talking about a workplace where any young woman with a sufficiently tartlike demeanor could reportedly enjoy the president's precious attentions, along with the career-counseling services of his closest friends."[52]

Seven months into the investigation of possible presidential felonies in the Jones case, the President's semen turned up on Monica Lewinsky's dress. Clinton then admitted to a grand jury and to the American public that he had had an "inappropriate" relationship (but not a sexual one!) with Lewinsky. This arguably complicated the position of those feminists who had defended him because they had believed his denials, or who at least had given him the benefit of believing them. Following Clinton's quasi-confession, some prominent feminists did express their disappointment in him. Describing Clinton's behavior as "disgusting" and "reprehensible," they seemed, however, to focus on the fact that he had had a (probably sexual) relationship with Lewinsky, not that he had probably lied about it in the Paula Jones case. And, even as they denounced the president's liaison, some feminists shifted the blame for it to Lewinsky. For example, in a CNBC interview with Brian Williams the day after the confession, Patricia Ireland warned: "This should be a lesson to young women not to use sex to try to enhance themselves in the workplace."[53] She repeated the lesson several days later on *Larry King*,

51. Alessandra Stanley, "Absence of Women's Outrage Sends Signal to Some Men," *New York Times*, January 31, 1998. The congresswoman spoke to the *Times* on condition of anonymity.

52. Barbara Ehrenreich, "The Week Feminists Got Laryngitis," *Time Magazine*, February 9, 1998.

53. Patricia Ireland, interview, *The News with Brian Williams*, CNBC, August 18, 1998.

saying that the "object lesson of all of this" is that "going into the workplace and using anything other than your ability . . . trying to use your sexual power . . . is not a good idea."[54] Here again, a feminist twisted a troubling fact about a man into a question of a woman's foul motives.

JUST ABOUT SEX

During the long year of inquiry into the Lewinsky matter, Clinton supporters conveyed their disdain for it with the refrain "it's just about sex." The phrase summarized several different claims: the Clinton-Lewinsky relationship was about sex, not harassment; sex is private; lies about sex are private; everybody lies about sex. If what we mean by "sex" is intimate activity that does not violate anyone's will, I agree with each one of these claims. But that is a big "if." Sometimes sex is a weapon of terror, or of power, or of shame. Sometimes people take the most private, intimate part of our selves and abuse it. To avenge this wrong requires inquiry into the acts that effectuate it: it requires inquiry into sex.

Clinton's defenders indulged in a dangerous syllogism when they insisted that privacy immunized the president's lies because the lies were about sex. They extended the syllogism when they insisted that the questions that elicited the lies should never have been asked because the questions were about sex. By this logic, privacy will always immunize inequality when discriminatory sexual conduct is inequality's source. By this logic, anyone who wishes to subordinate women should use sex as his means to do so.

The president's defenders, among them feminists, turned the subject of his alleged deceptions — sex — into excuses for committing those deceptions in a legal proceeding. Defending the president in this way, feminists effaced Paula Jones's charge that he had solicited sex from her in violation of her will and dignity. Further, they called "pattern and practice" inquiry into question, equated the appearance of consent in sex with proof of it, and strengthened the wall of pri-

54. Patricia Ireland, roundtable discussion, *Larry King*, CNN, August 21, 1998.

vacy behind which some women's consent counts for little. These developments could disarm women before sexual harassment law.

The starting point for the feminist defense of the president against perjury and obstruction of justice charges was that his relationship with Monica Lewinsky had been consensual. Gloria Steinem, for example, made this point soon after we first heard Lewinsky's name in January 1998. According to the *New York Times*, while Steinem noted the "suspicious power difference" between a middle-aged president and a young White House intern, she asserted "that 21-year-olds were old enough to 'say yes or no.'"[55] Two months later, she elaborated the point in an op-ed piece for the *Times:* "there is no evidence to suggest that Ms. Lewinsky's will was violated.... [w]elcome sexual behavior is about as relevant to sexual harassment as borrowing a car is to stealing one."[56] Patricia Ireland also expressed this view early on, telling ABC's Sam Donaldson that "if the president had a sexual relation with Monica Lewinsky, it was consensual.... If there is a pattern, it appears to be a pattern of consensual sex."[57]

By August, when it became clear that the president had had some kind of sexual contact with Lewinsky, many feminists pointed to the apparently consensual nature of the contact to condemn the Independent Counsel's sustained inquiries into it. For example, Sandy Bernard, president of the American Association of University Women, maintained that "no matter how much we despise his actions, this is not a case of sexual harassment."[58] Patricia Ireland issued a statement that "consensual sex is not illegal harassment."[59] A month later, prominent feminists including Betty Friedan, Eleanor Smeal, and the leaders of a number of women's groups joined ranks to denounce impeachment proceedings as "sexual McCarthyism," or

55. Bob Herbert, "The Feminist Dilemma," *New York Times*, January 29, 1998.

56. Gloria Steinem, "Feminists and the Clinton Question." The argument appeared in longer form in Gloria Steinem, "Yes Means Yes, No Means No: Why Sex Scandals Don't Mean Sexual Harassment."

57. Patricia Ireland, interview, *This Week*, ABC, February 1, 1998.

58. Statement of Sandy Bernard, President, American Association of University Women, PR Newswire, September 23, 1998.

59. "Statement of NOW President Patricia Ireland in Response to Reports of Clinton Testimony," press release, August 17, 1998.

an inquisition into a sexual affair that was nobody's business.[60] Meanwhile, writing in the *New York Times*, Anita Hill drew a distinction between her own allegations of sexual harassment against Clarence Thomas and allegations of a Clinton-Lewinsky "office affair." To equate the two, she said, "is to trivialize issues of sexual predation that women face in the workplace and on the street."[61] During the question-and-answer phase of Clinton's impeachment trial, five Democratic women senators reiterated this consent defense when they jointly asked: "Has Ms. Lewinsky ever claimed the relationship was other than consensual?"[62]

Feminists and other Clinton defenders were right to insist that consensual sex is not in itself sexual harassment, even if it happens in the workplace. But they were wrong to insist that a workplace affair is shielded from scrutiny just because it appears to be consensual. For one thing, a consensual workplace relationship between a superior and a subordinate can become sexual harassment if it creates a hostile environment for third parties. But more important, it *is* sexual harassment if what appears to be consent turns out to be acquiescence. A plaintiff seeking pattern evidence cannot distinguish consent from acquiescence — and thus cannot determine a pattern — until she receives truthful answers to questions the court allows her to ask.

Among the questions a plaintiff needs to ask pattern witnesses is whether each welcomed the sexual conduct the defendant directed toward her. This information cannot be surmised or assumed, even if a witness seems to be in a relationship with the defendant. Like Mechelle Vinson, the plaintiff in *Meritor*, some women may submit to sexual requests from their supervisors, rather than resist or refuse them. To outsiders, submission may look like consent. But women may submit because they feel they have to, not because they welcome the sex and in spite of the fact that they are emotionally or physically

60. Deborah Zabarenko, "'Sexual McCarthyism' if Clinton Ousted," Reuters, September 24, 1998; "Feminist Steinem Says Censure Clinton," Reuters, September 29, 1998.

61. Anita Hill, "The Thomas Lesson," *New York Times*, September 28, 1998.

62. Senators Boxer (D-California), Feinstein (D-California), Landrieu (D-Louisiana), Mikulski (D-Maryland), and Murray (D-Washington) posed the question during trial proceedings on January 23, 1999.

injured by it. Because the appearance of consent can conceal sexual harassment, the judge in Paula Jones's case authorized her to discover pattern evidence even from women who may have submitted to Clinton. The whole country now knows that Monica Lewinsky didn't merely submit to sex with the president; she welcomed it. This might have attenuated Lewinsky's relevance as a pattern witness had the Jones case gone to trial. On the other hand, Lewinsky's story might have corroborated a Clinton pattern of using female office help to get his jollies. Either way, Lewinsky's desire doesn't excuse the fact that the president lied about her to Paula Jones.

The "just about sex" defense, sustained over twelve months, divorced the Lewinsky issue from its context in the Jones case. It was easy for the Clinton camp to isolate the Lewinsky issue from the Jones case, because nobody gave a damn about Paula Jones. Almost seamlessly, the subject changed from lies in a sexual harassment proceeding to lies about an affair. The media eased this transition with its endless yammering from day one of the Lewinsky story about what kind of sex the president might have had with the intern. The House of Representatives, in a bipartisan vote, unwittingly completed the transition in September 1998 when it decided to publish the Independent Counsel's report — sight unseen — with its sexually graphic testimony from Monica Lewinsky.

That Lewinsky's testimony included sexual details was not unusual given that she was a witness in a case involving sex: prosecutors in rape cases seek similar details, for example, because they have to establish that penetration took place; plaintiffs in sexual harassment cases reveal such details when they describe what their harassers did to them. Nonetheless, Clinton's defenders denounced the Lewinsky evidence as "shameful," "pornographic," and "salacious," again drawing attention to presidential sex and away from alleged presidential perjury. With the president's insisting that whatever "contact" he had had with Lewinsky was not sex because it had been one-way — he took but never gave — the spotlight on the Clinton-Lewinsky affair fixed on sex.

However painful and embarrassing the national focus on his sexual affair may have been to the president and his family, it probably saved his presidency. The focus on his affair — on what he and Monica did together — permitted Clinton and his defenders to claim that legitimate legal questions about his sexual conduct toward women subordinates in the workplace actually were illegitimate political questions about sex.

Clinton's defense team drummed this message home throughout his impeachment and trial. During the House impeachment hearings, for example, Congressman Barney Frank (D-Massachusetts) led the defense of the president with variations on this point: "we have the following charge against Bill Clinton: he had a private, consensual affair and lied about it . . . the central charge . . . has to do with Mr. Clinton's denial that he touched Ms. Lewinsky in certain places for the purposes of causing gratification . . . this is about who touched whom where."[63] Congressman John Conyers (D-Michigan), the ranking Democrat on the House Judiciary Committee, declared that our "personal sex life is personal" and decried the impeachment inquiry for prying into "private sexual behavior."[64] Culminating the president's opening defense in the Senate trial, former Arkansas Senator Dale Bumpers told the president's jury that "it's about sex" — about a "breach of his marriage vows . . . not a breach of the public trust."[65] Feminists in the House and in the Senate underscored the message, declaring the president's affair to be "immoral," "repugnant," and "reprehensible," but not impeachable.[66]

63. Congressman Barney Frank (D-Massachusetts), comments during the House Judiciary Committee's debate on Impeachment Article I, December 11, 1998, partially quoted in "Excerpts from the Judiciary Committee's Debate on Article I," New York Times, December 12, 1998; also quoted in "Presidential Peace of Mind," http://www.search.washingtonpost.com/wp-srv/Wplate/1998-12-10/1781-121098-idx.html.

64. Congressman John Conyers (D-Michigan), opening statement in the House Judiciary Committee debate on articles of impeachment, December 10, 1998.

65. "Bumpers Defends the President," text of Senator Bumpers's speech reprinted from the Congressional Record, January 21, 1999, http://www.washingtonpost.com/wpsrv/politics/special/clinton/stories/bumperstext012199.htm.

66. These comments were repeated as catechism. For examples, see Congresswoman Sheila Jackson Lee (D-Texas), opening statement, House impeachment hearings, excerpted in the Washington Post, December 12, 1998;

The "just about sex" defense emphasized what Clinton did or didn't do with Monica Lewinsky, rather than what he said or didn't say about it in the Jones case. This permitted him to appeal to our sense of privacy, as he did in his August 1998 confession of an "inappropriate" relationship. Appeals to privacy properly excite us to defend our personal freedom. They also understandably impel us to guard our personal pain jealously, such as when we are hurt by adultery. But appeals to privacy can also manipulate us into shielding acts of inequality from public view. When President Clinton told us that his sex lies were "nobody's business," he exploited a cherished political value to deprive a sexual harassment plaintiff a fair proceeding in her case against him.

Feminists abetted the president's efforts to sheathe himself in sexual and family privacy, variously insisting that even a president's "sex life" is private, that "it's between Bill and Hillary," and that "people voted for [him] knowing he wasn't perfect in his personal life."[67] On the face of it, these claims are indisputable: sex and adultery are private. But the sex in sexual harassment is not "just sex," but also power, and power exudes public consequences. Nor is the sex in sexual harassment private, even if one of its implications is adultery. It would be very strange indeed if our sexual harassment laws exempted married defendants from truth-telling because their wives might find out about their adultery.

Adopting the perspective of the married harasser (Bill Clinton) and his wife (Hillary Clinton), many feminists stranded sexually harassed women behind the wall of privacy. For thirty years, feminists

<hr />

Congresswoman Rosa DeLauro (D-Connecticut), floor statement opposing impeachment, excerpted in the *New York Times*, December 19, 1998; Congresswoman Nita Lowey (D-New York), floor statement opposing impeachment, excerpted in the *New York Times*, December 19, 1998. The censure resolution prepared for consideration in the Senate by Senator Dianne Feinstein (D-California) began by condemning the President's "immoral" behavior.

67. Barbara Vobjeda, "Key Constituency Reverses Itself"; Tony Perry, "Boxer Touts Clinton Achievements, Rejects Calls for His Resignation," *Los Angeles Times*, August 22, 1998; Judy Mann, "What Has Clinton Wrought? Four Women Reflect," *Washington Post*, August 26, 1998; Zabarenko, "'Sexual McCarthyism' If Clinton Ousted."

have argued that "the personal is political." The idea is that women have been unequal not only because the laws have made us so, but also because private acts and relations have enforced social inequality. Private inequalities ranging from the sexual division of labor to rape have public effects, among them the muting of women's public voice and the capping of our economic opportunity. Hence, feminists have fought for public remedies for private inequalities — domestic violence legislation, for example — in the process illuminating the nexus between private conduct and political power.

Bill Clinton's feminist allies disconnected the personal from the political when they insisted that the investigation into Clinton's alleged lies and cover-up in Paula Jones's sexual harassment case was an invasion of Clinton's sexual and family privacy. It would be disturbing enough had they offered the privacy shield to an alleged sexual offender who performed his injuries on a friend or a wife behind the closed doors of his home. But in this case, feminists argued that potentially unlawful sexual conduct performed *in public*— in the workplace — should escape public, or legal, review. Surrendering equality to sexual privacy, they propelled public discussion of sexual harassment backwards to the 1970s, when courts insisted that sexual harassment was about sex, not about inequality.

WHERE DO WE GO FROM HERE?

From within and without, feminism has endured considerable criticism in recent years, in part for its authorship of sexual harassment law. Variously labeled prudes, puritans, and the sex police, feminists have been accused both of suppressing women's sexual agency and of denying men's sexual freedom. Feminists certainly gave the lie to these charges when so many invoked Monica Lewinsky's sexual agency to defend Bill Clinton's sexual freedom. But they also traded away Paula Jones's right to enjoy *her* sexual agency and Bill Clinton's obligation not to abuse his sexual freedom. More important, they traded Paula Jones's right to hold Bill Clinton accountable when he abused his sexual freedom.

That right is the crux of sexual harassment law. Contrary to widespread opinion, sexual harassment law does not regulate sexuality, ban romance, punish flirtation, or even discourage sex. Many employers choose to do these things to minimize exposure to liability, preferring the quick fix of blanket prohibitions to the costlier and more time-consuming work of teaching equality. But the law does not require such prohibitions. What the law does is to give targets a remedy — a cause for civil action — when their agency has been impaired, their personhood shamed, or their opportunity compromised by someone who imposes sex or sexual abuse on them in the workplace or at school. By giving women a basis for avenging sexualized inequality, the law establishes the expectation that the people with whom we work and learn will not use sex to subvert equality.

Meeting the expectations of the law — avoiding women's need to use it — should not be difficult. How hard is it to keep your pants on at work? How hard is it to keep your hands off an employee's breasts? How hard is it to save your requests for oral sex for the person with whom you are intimately involved? How hard is it to call an employee by her own name rather than by the name of a female body part or of a female dog? How hard is it to think about what the other person wants before inflicting your behaviors on them?

The conduct suggested by these questions may sound absurd, but such conduct is commonly reported in sexual harassment lawsuits. Far from being extreme or oppressive, sexual harassment law actually permits such conduct unless its target complains about it, for the law prohibits only conduct that is *unwelcome*. Moreover, even when a target complains, sexual harassment law does not necessarily secure her relief. What stands between sexual harassment law and women's vindication is that the law operates within a regime of disbelief.

A year of political conflict over Bill Clinton, Paula Jones, and Monica Lewinsky strengthened the regime, augmenting long-standing conservative political hostility to sexual harassment plaintiffs with new liberal suspicions of them. Bipartisan, bipolar support for the regime was never clearer than when many feminists declared Bill Clinton the *victim* of his own alleged sexual misconduct and when they trumped his target's right to pursue legal redress with his right to privacy.

Many feminists defended Clinton because they were reluctant to aid conservatives in their opportunistic use of sexual harassment law to bring down a president who was "doing a good job for women."[68] This calculus was freighted with betrayals and risks. Feminists may have helped to preserve the Clinton presidency, but in exchange they ceded the moral high ground in the politics of sexual harassment. They may have helped Clinton reclaim his privacy, but in exchange they saved a president who has no respect for anyone's privacy other than his own.

One of the policy achievements Clinton most likes to tout is welfare reform. Although enacted by a Republican Congress, welfare reform began as Clinton's initiative, became law with his signature, and includes provisions he espoused. Among those provisions are tough paternity establishment and child support requirements that compel poor unmarried mothers to answer the government's questions about their sex lives. If they refuse, they can be denied medicaid or welfare. If they lie, they can be prosecuted for fraud. Indeed, if a welfare recipient misleads the government about anything it wants to know, she can be — and often is — prosecuted for fraud.

Welfare reform was one of Clinton's policies toward and about women. In fact, it was his principal women's policy, as most of the policies he has accepted credit for actually were initiated and guided through Congress by feminist legislators — the Family and Medical Leave Act, for example, and the Violence Against Women Act. Clinton's welfare reform tramples poor single mothers' rights, including their privacy rights, enforcing their inequality as citizens and as women. This is "doing a good job for women"?

Even were he women's policy messiah, would that exempt him from personally abiding by the law? Feminists insisted on separating the personal Clinton from the political one, as if he didn't act politically to advance himself personally. Yet, by his political actions toward Paula Jones and every other woman with a story to tell, he protected his personal stature in Paula Jones's case against him. And by

68. E.g., Anita Hill, interview, *Late Edition*, CNN, August 16, 1998; Patricia Ireland, interview, *Late Edition*, August 16, 1998; Kathy Spillar, National Coordinator, Feminist Majority Foundation, quoted in Barbara Vobejda, "Key Constituency Reverses Itself"; Betty Friedan, interview, *Newstand: Time*.

his personal actions in the Jones case, he protected his political grasp on the presidency.

The result, I think, is a precarious political future for sexual harassment law, putting both accomplished and still-needed improvements in the law in jeopardy. Most feminists remain staunchly committed to fighting sexual harassment, notwithstanding their defense of President Clinton. However, in the course of their defense, outspoken feminists may have diluted their own cause with restrictive definitions of what sexual harassment "really" is. As the main public voice for gender justice, feminist leaders play an important role educating the public about how women experience inequality and what we want done about it. Unfortunately, their message to the public during the criminal investigation, then impeachment, of the president may harden the public's disdain toward the issue of sexual harassment and toward laws the public thinks "have gone too far in making common interactions between employees into cases of sexual harassment."[69]

Feminist leaders also give cues to Democrats — as they did in the wake of the Hill-Thomas hearings, when Democrats fell all over themselves to denounce sexual harassment. In this instance, feminists' participation in the "just about sex" defense may give Democrats license to curtail "pattern and practice" inquiry in sexual harassment cases. There's no reason to believe that Republicans — once so hostile to a monetary damages remedy for "frivolous" sexual harassment lawsuits — have become converts to sexual harassment law. In fact, the Clinton scandal may have invigorated conservative groups' efforts to weaken the law. Already, the Independent Women's Forum has challenged NOW to join in repudiating some of the law's basic elements, including the use of "pattern and practice" evidence, for example.[70] So feminists who feared association with Paula Jones because of her right-wing friends may see Democrats and Republicans on the same side of efforts to roll back sexual harassment law.

69. According to a CNN poll in March 1998, 52 percent of American women and 57 percent of American men held this view.

70. "Reaction to NOW/Feminist News Conference; Independent Women's Forum Calls for Reforms," PR Newswire, December 15, 1998.

In addition to these idle speculations are some concrete issues. Although the Supreme Court strengthened employer liability for sexual harassment under Title VII in 1998, it also severely limited the liability of school districts under Title IX. In *Gebser v. Lago Vista Independent School District*, a slim majority of the Court precluded a suit for monetary damages by a student who had been harassed by one of her teachers.[71] Part of the Court's argument was that Title IX lacks Title VII's language implicating "agents" of institutions governed by the law. Absent agency principles, the Court said, Title IX does not confer liability on school districts for sexual harassment and thus does not support an individual claim for damages — unless a school district official with authority to remedy the situation knows about it and is "deliberately indifferent" to it. This narrow construction of Title IX's sexual harassment remedies is especially disturbing given the acute power imbalance between teachers and students.

As with all statutory rights and remedies, this decision can be corrected by Congress. Congress corrected the Court's interpretation of Title VII in the Civil Rights Act of 1991; it can likewise correct *Gebser* by amending Title IX now. Fearing the expense, school districts don't want liability for sexual harassment under Title IX, so they will undoubtedly present a formidable opposition to any change. Meanwhile, many Republicans, including the Speaker of the House of Representatives, are frustrated by Title IX generally, mainly because gender equity conditions for federal educational assistance interfere with men's grip on school sports. Against this opposition, will feminists and Democrats have the moral and political currency to correct *Gebser*?

Other issues of immediate concern include making sure sexual harassment law works for economically vulnerable women. The pain of harassment is as intense as it is various: sexual harassment is not unique to particular women, though each of us endures it uniquely. However, the cost of harassment is uniquely high for women who risk destitution if they complain about it. Low-wage women workers, including mothers on welfare, are particularly vulnerable in this way. Those who quit their jobs cannot collect unemployment insur-

71. *Gebser v. Lago Vista Independent School District*, 524 U.S. 274 (1998).

ance unless they can persuade their states that their sexual harassment was "good cause" for quitting. Those who need food stamps have to prove that their sexual harassment was "good cause" for becoming unemployed. Those who need welfare would do best to suffer their sexual harassment if their only alternative is to quit their required work activity, deplete their time limits, and lose their families' benefits.

For these women, some of whom Clinton's people might call "trailer trash," new policy initiatives are needed along with stronger enforcement of existing law. Welfare, food stamps, and unemployment insurance policies should be amended to define sexual harassment as "good cause" for leaving a job. Federal policy should suspend penalties and time limits for welfare mothers who leave work because of sexual harassment. States should be required to guarantee Title VII safeguards to all workfare participants and to require strict Title VII compliance of private employers who hire welfare recipients.

Even if these changes could be accomplished, however, their effect on women's lives would still depend on the strength of each woman's word. Sexual harassment provisions are useless to women whose sexual harassment is not believed. And they are useless to women who will not tell of their harassment because the personal and political costs of doing so remain extreme.

Index

Clinton, Bill (*continued*)
Jones's personal life and, 107; "just about sex" as defense of, 129–35; Packwood and Thomas compared to, 123; pattern of sexual conduct of, 116, 124–26, 131–32; possible perjury and cover-up by, 116–17, 124–25, 132; reactions of, 78–79, 116; VAWA signed by, 107–8; welfare reform of, 137. *See also* impeachment; *Jones v. Clinton*; regime of disbelief
Clinton, Hillary Rodham, 117, 134
CNBC (station), 128–29
CNN (station), 38, 123, 138n. 69
"Condemning Sexual Harassment" (Senate Resolution), 52n. 46, 99
Conley, Frances, 82
conservatives: blamed for Jones's case, 120; blamed for Lewinsky's testimony, 117; on men's sexual conduct vs. women's rights, 37–39; sexual harassment claims supported by, 2, 4, 136–38
Conyers, John, 133
Corne, Jane, 25, 43, 48, 51
Cornell University, 20–22, 25–26
Corne v. Bausch and Lomb, Inc.: appealed, 48; mentioned, 25n. 50, 43n. 16; obtuseness of decision, 46; as precedent, 44, 45
Coughlin, Lt. Paula, 101
courts: cases rejected by, 24–25; on civil rights and sexual harassment, 39–40; on disparate impact theory, 86–87, 89–90; on employer liability, 70–71, 88–89; on establishing discrimination, 72–73; evidence on women's character allowed by, 67–69; on frequency and type of conduct, 71–72; on hostile environment concept, 30, 55–66; reasonableness standard used by, 34, 72–75; on sexual intimidation, 54–55, 58–59; on

women's reactions to men's sexual conduct, 52–53, 66–69. *See also* sexual harassment law; U.S. Supreme Court; *specific cases*
Craig v. Boren, 93n. 51
credibility: emphasis on, 32–33, 82–83; improved with pattern and practice evidence, 124; media on, 4–5; motivation and, 125–26; politics of, 115. *See also* regime of disbelief
criminal rape shield, 104–6, 111
culture, of sexualized inequality, 77

Danforth, John, 98
dating contracts, 38–39
Davis, Martha, 120–21
DeCrow, Karen, 26
Delaney v. City of Hampton, Virginia, 106n. 91
DeLauro, Rosa, 133–34n. 66
Democratic women, ambivalence about sexual harassment law, 32
Dershowitz, Alan, 118n. 16
DeVane, Geneva, 25, 43, 48, 51
Diaz v. Pan American World Airways, Inc., 22n. 41, 88n. 34
disability plans, 22n. 43
discrimination: categorical type of, 87–88; courts on establishing, 72–73; definition of employment, 55–56; intentional, 87–88, 91–94, 97–98; proof of, 88–91. *See also* race discrimination; sex discrimination
disparate impact theory: civil rights bill's impact on, 97–98; class action suits and, 86, 89–90; core harm in, 50; stiffer requirements in, 86–87
District of Columbia Department of Corrections, 59
Dole, Bob, 98n. 61, 107
Donaldson, Sam, 130
Dooling, Richard, 85n. 25
Dothard v. Rawlinson, 22n. 41, 22–23n. 44, 86, 88n. 34

feminism (*continued*)
success for, 105, 111; premises of,
6–7, 118–19. *See also* feminists
Feminist Majority, 121
feminists: as ambivalent about sexual
harassment law, 32–33; Clinton
defended by, 118–29, 133–38; on
credibility, 4–5; Hill's treatment
and, 84–85, 98; Jones disparaged
by, 118–25, 128, 129; on *Jones v.
Clinton* decision, 31; "just about
sex" defense by, 133–35;
Lewinsky disparaged by, 127–
29; pattern and practice evidence
trivialized by, 124; sexual
harassment law compromised
by, 121–29, 135–40; sexual
harassment law criticized by, 3,
41–42; sexual harassment law
dismantled by, 129–35; on Title
VII's goal, 96; violence and
inequality linked by, 111–13;
Willey disparaged by, 125–27.
See also feminism
Ferraro, Geraldine, 127
*Firefighters Institute for Racial
Equality v. City of St. Louis*, 57n. 59
flight attendants, 47, 88
Flowers, Gennifer, 128
Frank, Barney, 133
Frank v. County of Hudson, 108n. 95,
109n. 98
Friedan, Betty, 121, 123, 130

Gates, Henry Louis, Jr., 41n. 12
*Gebser v. Lago Vista Independent
School District*, 32n. 70, 33n. 76,
139
General Electric Co. v. Gilbert, 22n. 43
Goodman, Ellen, 4–5
Gray, C. Boyden, 83
Greenberger, Marcia, 84
Griggs v. Duke Power Co., 56, 86,
87n. 32, 89, 90
Guardian Weekly, on Jones's case,
123
Guidelines on Sexual Harassment in

the Workplace (EEOC), 60, 61,
63, 65

Hall v. Gus Construction Co., 23n. 47
harassers: sex used by, 23–24;
structural advantages of, 79, 110;
tactics of, 2–3. *See also* power;
regime of disbelief; *specific
individuals*
Harris, Teresa, 74
Harris v. Forklift Systems, Inc.:
departure from, 119, 125;
mentioned, 28n. 59, 40n. 11;
on psychological well-being, 74;
threshold and, 75
Hatch, Orrin, 82n. 15, 83
Henson, Barbara, 61
Henson v. City of Dundee: affirmed,
65; appealed, 61; on employer's
responsibility, 63; mentioned,
40n. 9; as precedent, 50n. 42, 66,
70; subjective standard in, 62–64;
on threshold, 70–71, 76
Hicks v. Gates Rubber Co., 23n. 47
Hill, Anita: Clinton on, 78–79;
courage of, 101; credibility of, 4,
82–83; feminist support for, 7,
118; on Jones's case, 31, 121; on
Lewinsky-Clinton affair, 131;
personal attacks on, 1–2, 83–85;
ten-year silence of, 82, 99–100
Hill-Thomas hearings: civil rights
bill and, 97; personal attacks in,
83–85; reason convened, 98;
women demoralized by, 5n. 15
Hodgson v. Robert Hall Clothes, Inc.,
23n. 45
Holtzman, Elizabeth, 105n. 87
Hopkins, Ann, 88–89
hostile environment: cases of, 53–
54, 119; components in, 57–61;
consensual relationship and, 131;
context of conduct in, 68–69;
defined as sex discrimination,
40–41, 54–55, 60–66, 122;
distinctions in, 29; distortion of,
119–20; employers as responsible

for, 61, 63, 70–71; employer's
liability in, 63, 114–15; feminists'
rejection of, 125, 129–35;
guidelines in, 61–62; legal
components of, 30–31;
psychological well-being in,
62, 73–75, 106–7, 119; public
acceptance of concept, 30; quid
pro quo harassment compared to,
61–62; race discrimination via,
55–57; statute of limitations issue
in, 81, 91; testimony on, 94–96;
threshold in, 30, 62–63, 68, 70–
71, 76, 103–4, 122–23. *See also*
employers
Hunter v. Allis-Chalmers Corp., 109–
10n. 101

impeachment: feminists'
denunciation of, 130; "just about
sex" defense in, 133–35; legal
system improvements and, 84–
85; questions in, 131
Independent Women's Forum, 138
individuals: civil actions as
possibility for, 111–13;
discrimination against, 88;
liability of, 93, 114n. 1; as source
of sexual harassment, 27
injunctions, enforceability of, 100
Ireland, Patricia: on Clinton's
admission, 128–29; on consent,
130; on credibility, 5, 32, 33,
125–26; on Jones's case, 120,
124–25
Isikoff, Michael, 2

Jackson, Jesse, 2
Jackson Lee, Sheila, 133–34n. 66
James v. Stockham Valves & Fittings,
57n. 57
*Johnson v. Railway Express Agency,
Inc.*, 92n. 49
Jones, Paula: accused of "sexual
McCarthyism," 118, 130–31;
credibility of, 4–5, 32; feminists'
disparagement of, 118–25, 128,

129; job-related loss issue and,
34–35; personal attacks on, 2, 7,
28; personal life of, 107. *See also
Jones v. Clinton*
Jones v. Clinton: appealed, 120; civil
sex offense shield and, 107n. 92;
Clinton's possible perjury and
obstruction of justice in, 117–18;
complaint in, 115–16; discovery
process in, 116, 124; dismissed,
119–20, 121; judicial argument
in, 30–31; pattern and practice
evidence in, 124–25, 129–32;
physical contact and, 108; politics
of, 113; quid pro quo harassment
concept used in, 30–31, 35;
transition in focus of, 132–33
*Jones v. Commander, Kansas Army
Ammunitions Plant*, 67n. 90
Jones v. Flagship International, 62n.
78
Jones v. Wesco Investments, 71n. 108

Katz, Deborah, 5
Kennedy, Edward, 98, 99
Kennelly, Barbara, 99n. 65
King, Larry, 6
Kresko v. Rulli, 68n. 93
Kristol, William, 83
Ku Klux Klan Act, 92–93

Larry King (television program), on
Clinton's admission, 128–29
Lewinsky, Monica: Clinton's
admission of relations with, 117–
18, 128–30; consensual relations
of, 131–32; feminists'
disparagement of, 127–29;
testimony in Jones's case, 108,
116–17, 124
Lewis, Ann, 126–27
liberals: ambivalence about sexual
harassment law, 32; feminists'
influence on, 138; on Jones, 34–
35; sexual harassment law
challenged by, 3, 4. *See also*
feminists

"personal is political," betrayal of, 135–40
Phillips, Nancy, 93–94
Phillips v. Martin Marietta Corp., 47n. 32
Phillips v. Smalley Maintenance Services, Inc., 109–10n. 101
Policy Guidance on Sexual Harassment (EEOC), 71
politics: battles lost in, 6–7; harassers' advantages in, 79, 110; men's sexual conduct vs. women's rights in, 37–42, 53; personal attacks in, 1–3, 7, 28, 83–85. *See also* conservatives; liberals; power; regime of disbelief
Posner, Richard, 72, 110
power: dismissed as factor, 130–35; liability linked to, 64; in sexual conduct, 39–42, 46; sexual extortion based in, 46–51; in sexual harassment, 24, 27, 115, 121–22; of supervisors, 47–51, 53–54. *See also* regime of disbelief
Pregnancy Discrimination Act (1978), 22n. 43
preventive measures, support for, 7
Price Waterhouse v. Hopkins, 88–89, 90
Priest v. Rotary, 69n. 98
prior acts evidence, 107
prison guards, 22–23n. 44
privacy: Clinton's vs. others', 137; "just about sex" rhetoric and, 129–35; women's civil rights vs. men's, 119
propensity, rules on, 103, 108–10
psychological well-being, in hostile environment concept, 62, 73–75, 106–7, 119
Public Service Electric and Gas Company, 45–46

Quayle, Dan, 83
quid pro quo harassment: cases involving, 30–31, 35, 42–51, 58–59, 116, 119; elements of, 29, 49–51, 54; employer's liability in, 63; hostile environment compared to, 61–62; limitations of, 51, 53–54; as sex discrimination, 40
Quindlen, Anna, 4

Rabidue, Vivienne, 73–74
Rabidue v. Osceola Refining Company, 73–75
race, intimidation based in, 54
race discrimination: banned, 55–56; damages for, 92–93, 96–97; examples of, 43, 56–57
racial harassment: court ruling on, 52; as precedent for law on sexual harassment, 54–57; sexual harassment compared to, 66
rape, prosecutions for, 105–6. *See also* criminal rape shield
reasonableness standard, 34, 72–75
Reed, JoAnn, 66–67n. 89
Reed v. Arlington Hotel Corporation, 56n. 56
Reed v. Shepard, 66–67n. 89
regime of disbelief: consolidation of, 115–19; description of, 77; "just about sex" used in, 129–35; sexual harassment law within, 136; tactics in, 127–28; women subordinated in, 79
Rehnquist, William, 106
respondeat superior, 48
Robinson, Lois, 95–96
Robinson v. Jacksonville Shipyards, Inc., 109–10n. 101
Rogers v. EEOC: on hostile environment, 55–57; mentioned, 52n. 47; as precedent, 57–58, 65

Sanchez v. Zabihi, et al., 106n. 90
Seinfeld (television program), 38
Senate: resolution of, 52n. 46, 99; sexual harassment office of, 91
Senate Judiciary Committee, ignorance of, 98–99. *See also* Hill-Thomas hearings
sex: consent vs. acquiescence in, 130–32; desire vs. expression of,

sex (*continued*)
53; involuntary vs. voluntary, 69;
Lewinsky matter as "just about,"
129–35; nature of, 27, 53; as
occupational qualification, 87–88;
as personal, 39, 43–46
sex discrimination: civil action for,
111–13, 136; definition of, 24–25,
40, 47–48; hostile environment
defined as, 40–41, 54–55, 60–
66, 122; inequality and, 34; legal
framework established, 22n. 41;
liabilities and, 93–94; questions
about, 22–23; sexual conduct
linked to, 39–42, 53, 61–62;
sexual extortion as, 47–51; sexual
harassment as, 40, 75, 122; sexual
intimidation as, 24–28, 54–55,
58–59; subjective injury and,
51–66
sexual assault, U.S. Code on,
108
sexual conduct: consent issue and,
130–32; context of, 68–69, 103;
discrimination in, 42–51, 60;
employer's knowledge of, 70–71,
114; as harassment, 66–75; as
meaningless, 62–63; unwelcome,
as sex discrimination, 37–42, 53,
61–62, 136; verbal vs. physical,
71–72, 108; welcome vs.
unwelcome, 69–70, 75, 103–
4; women's reactions to men's,
46, 52–53, 58, 66–69
sexual harassment: attitudes toward,
78–79, 82–83, 138; cost of, 139–
40; definition of, 23–24, 28–30,
40, 52, 66–75; as discrimination,
40, 75, 122; economic loss from,
58; injunctions against, 100;
intent of, 27–28, 60, 67; making
visible, 25–27; "perfect cases" of,
32–33; personal example of, 8–
20; public awareness increased,
101–2; rates of, 26–27, 79–80;
as routine, 37–39; statute of
limitations on, 80–81, 91;
subjective effects of, 51–66, 122–

23; tactics in, 21, 24, 28, 53–54,
60; women's response to, 46, 52–
53, 58, 66–69. *See also* hostile
environment; quid pro quo
harassment
sexual harassment law: ambivalence
toward, 32, 33; challenges to,
3; components of, 3–4, 7;
compromised by feminists, 121–
29, 135–40; consensus on, 28;
core harm in, 50; criticism of, 3,
37–39, 41–42; dismantled by
feminists, 129–35; enforcement
of, 31; on frequency and type of
conduct, 71–72; limitations and
contradictions of, 7, 31–32, 33–
36, 41–42, 45, 65; reasonableness
standard in, 34, 72–75;
strengthened, 34–35, 40, 76–
77, 85n. 25; threshold in, 29, 62–
63, 68, 70–71, 76, 103–4, 122–
23; on women's response to
harassment, 66–69. *See also*
evidence
sexual harassment policy, 66n. 87,
76–77
sexually harassed women: barriers
for, 80–82, 96, 104, 110, 134–
36; character and behavior of,
67–69, 102–7; choices of, 99–
100; compensation for, 92–99;
demoralization of, 5; disparaged
by feminists, 118–29; incentives
for, 101–2, 104, 115; as
percentage of women, 7n. 20,
26–27, 77, 79, 100; personal
attacks on, 1–3, 7, 28, 83–85;
"reasonable" type of, 72–75;
social costs for, 81–82, 104,
110; vulnerability of, 139–40.
See also credibility; motivation;
psychological well-being
"sexual McCarthyism," use of, 118,
130–31
Shea v. Galaxie Lumber &
Construction Company, Ltd., 110n.
103
Simpson, Alan, 82n. 15, 83

U.S. Supreme Court (*continued*)
offense shield, 106; on Clinton's
motion to dismiss, 116; on
employer liability, 139; on hostile
environment, 30, 64–66; on
mixed-motive case, 88–91; on
psychological injury, 74, 119; on
racial discrimination, 92n. 49; on
reasonableness standard, 74–75;
on sex discrimination definition,
40; sexual harassment defined by,
29–30; sexual harassment law
strengthened by, 34–35; on
threshold, 122. *See also specific
cases, e.g., Meritor Savings Bank v.
Vinson*
USA Today, on responsibility, 6

Vermett v. Hough, 66–67n. 89
Vinson, Mechelle, 65, 69, 131
Vinson v. Taylor, 64–66, 69
Violence Against Women Act
(VAWA, 1994): civil action as
possibility under, 112–13;
components of, 104–5, 111;
passage of, 107–8; support for,
137
Violent Crime Control and Law
Enforcement Act (1994), 107–8

Wall Street Journal: on employer's
defense, 102–3; on Hill, 1
Wangler v. Hawaiian Electric Co., Inc.,
103n. 81
Wards Cove Packing Co. v. Atonio, 86,
89–90
Washington Post, on Paula Jones, 2
*Watts v. New York City Police
Department*, 71n. 108
Webb v. Hyman, 109–10n. 101
*Weihaupt v. American Medical
Association*, 4n. 9

Weiss v. Amoco Oil Co., 68n. 94
welfare reform, debacle of, 137
*West Virginia University Hospitals v.
Casey*, 90n. 42
Willey, Kathleen, 108, 123, 125–27
Williams, Brian, 128
Williams, Diane, 26n. 56, 47–48, 51
Williams v. Saxbe et al., 26n. 56, 47–
48, 49
Wimberly v. Shoney's Inc., 63n. 80
Wolf v. Burum, 71n. 111
women: exclusion of, 41–42;
hostility toward, 28; right to
be free of gender-motivated
violence, 111–13; strength of
sexual harassment law and, 35–
36. *See also* mothers; sexually
harassed women
Women's Legal Defense Fund, 34,
56n. 55, 58, 96
Women's Rights Litigation Clinic,
48
Wood, Carmita: appeal of, 33;
sexual harassment of, 20–22, 25;
support for, 25–27
workers: barriers for, 88–90; right
to jury trial, 97–98; statute of
limitations for, 81, 91. *See also*
employment; federal workers
Working Women United (Ithaca),
25–26
Wright, Susan Webber: case
dismissed by, 119–20, 121;
criticism of, 121n. 25; discovery
process and, 116; Lewinsky's
evidence excluded by, 124–25;
quid pro quo harassment used by,
30–31, 32, 35; testimony allowed
by, 108

*Young v. Southwestern Savings and
Loan Association*, 4n. 9